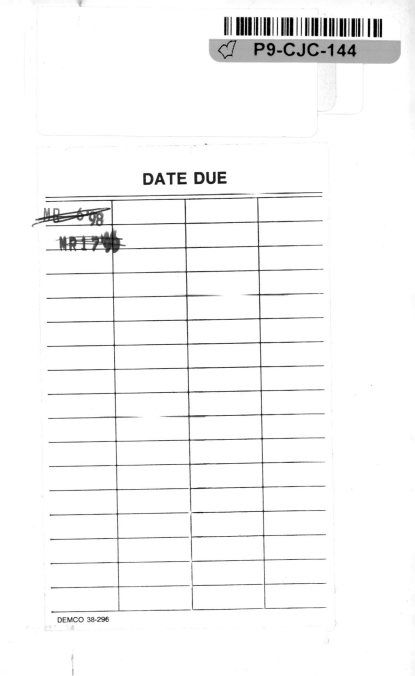

Teachers College • Columbia University
Comparative Education Studies
General Editor • George Z. F. Bereday

FINANCING SOVIET SCHOOLS

By HAROLD J. NOAH

CHARLES E. MERRIAM'S
THE MAKING OF CITIZENS

Introduction and Notes by GEORGE Z. F. BEREDAY

EDUCATION AND DEVELOPMENT IN WESTERN
EUROPE, THE UNITED STATES, AND
THE U.S.S.R.: A COMPARATIVE STUDY

By RAYMOND POIGNANT

VICTOR COUSIN AS A
COMPARATIVE EDUCATOR

By WALTER VANCE BREWER

FRESHMEN AND SOPHOMORES ABROAD:
COMMUNITY COLLEGES AND OVERSEAS
ACADEMIC PROGRAMS

By GERHARD HESS

FRESHMEN AND SOPHOMORES ABROAD:

COMMUNITY COLLEGES

AND

OVERSEAS ACADEMIC PROGRAMS

FRESHMEN AND SOPHOMORES ABROAD

Community Colleges and Overseas Academic Programs

GERHARD HESS

TEACHERS COLLEGE   COLUMBIA UNIVERSITY

NEW YORK AND LONDON   1982

Published by Teachers College Press,
1234 Amsterdam Avenue, New York,
New York 10027

Library of Congress Cataloging in Publication Data

Hess, Gerhard, 1929–
    Freshmen and sophomores abroad.

    (Comparative education studies)
    Bibliography: p.
    Includes index.
    1. Foreign study.   2.   Community colleges—
United States—Curricula.   3.   International
education.   4.   Comparative education.   I.
Title.   II.   Series.
LB2376.H47   1982   370.19′62   82-5901
                                                        AACR2

ISBN: 0-8077-2727-X

The quotations in chapter 2 from "Position Paper"
by the International Studies and World Affairs
Committee of the State University of New York
were used by permission of the Office of International Programs of the State University of
New York.

The quotation in chapter 4 from the *International/
Intercultural Consortium Brochure* was used by
permission of the International/Intercultural
Consortium of the American Association of
Community and Junior Colleges.

Manufactured in the United States of America

87   86   85   84   83   82   1   2   3   4   5   6

Contents

Foreword

The tenth volume of the COLUMBIA COMPARATIVE EDUCATION STUDIES devotes its attention to a previously unexplored area. Seven of these studies have attempted to preserve rare and important comparative education classics in contemporary volumes. The eighth work, by Passin on Japan, provided the only venture into a "one country" study, a field that since then has been preempted by the Pergamon Press. The ninth book, by Poignant, dealt with the theme of current modernization in European countries. That book, bolstered by the addition of Japan, now has been reprinted in Europe.

This volume is the account of substantial technical efforts to organize programs overseas. The book presents an important description of how the idea to send abroad students of freshman and sophomore standing originated and became firmly established in a dynamic community college setting.

Dr. Hess, a creator of this movement, was encouraged to put it in print and to show in detail the practical mechanics and methods by which such activities can be deployed. It is not surprising that these efforts were successful at the level of community colleges, which constitute a splendidly vibrant sector of American higher education today. The development of such a program represents international education and administrative process, both of which deserve to be emphasized in comparative education.

It is perhaps a small but powerful portent of a new era—a dream that all schoolchildren and college students can be socialized to the extent of belonging to a global rather than merely a national community.

Acknowledgments belong to two leaders in the field of international education: Dr. James A. Perkins, President of the International Council for Educational Development, who helped with the completion of this last volume of the series; and Dr. Robert L. Payton, President of the Exxon Education Foundation, who saw fit to support this topic with a generous grant covering the cost of publication.

George Z. F. Bereday

Introduction

This book presents the mechanics of establishing and maintaining a viable series of overseas academic programs at the community-college level. Several questions, general as well as specific, have to be asked: Is it appropriate at all for community college students to have some international exposure? If so, how deep should such involvement be in educational institutions designed to keep students for only two years before passing them on to other colleges or into the labor market? Other specific questions examine the practicalities. They evaluate the processes of developing international programs within the constraints inherent in community colleges, their financial limitations, and programmatic rules.

Throughout, this work provides extensive descriptive material on the operational details of developing overseas academic programs. The difficulties in mounting such programs are inherent and multiplied in colleges with two-year curricula, which usually do not provide the flexibility to incorporate a one-semester academic experience in another country. The material carries implicit guidelines for a policy on whether a community college should offer international training at all, to what extent it should do so, and how these guidelines can be successfully implemented. Does a community college, a self-contained single institution, have enough of a basis to develop international programs, or should several such colleges band together in a specialized network, so that they may combine benefits of specialization with the power of the joint use of resources? The impact upon the faculty, the students, and the surrounding community is of special significance in a milieu which, by definition, may otherwise be thought of as regional in scope, concerned narrowly with local affairs, and frequently conservative enough to fear the effects of international exposure.

On the national level, a multicollege, multistate consortium has begun to apply the experiences gained at one community college. On the international level, the development and implementation of the overseas academic programs described in this book have required developing a system of contacts, consultations, and negotiations with a wide variety of institutions and several overseas governments. The result was a network which, once established, has assured the success of the program and become a model of operation within the American community college field.

As a result of these successes, an affirmative answer is implied throughout this work to the question whether the intellectual extra dimension inherent in overseas programs should be an indispensable part of *all* levels of higher education.

FRESHMEN AND SOPHOMORES ABROAD:

COMMUNITY COLLEGES

AND

OVERSEAS ACADEMIC PROGRAMS

1. History of Internationalism in Institutions of Higher Learning

Internationalism in higher education is as old as higher education itself. International education has constituted one of the most important elements in institutions of higher education in all countries and at all times.

Most significant in any historical evaluation of higher education is the fact that many of its institutions catered to very young students. By definition, "universitas" means universality, and the early appearance of the term *university* testifies to the awareness that all intellectual interests have global roots and must be treated from the perspective of humanity as a whole. This feeling for the unity of mankind has been present wherever scholars and thinkers have congregated, even before universities as we know them today made their appearance. In the academic thought of the East as well as the West, it was recognized that there are no national boundaries.

From earliest times, even very young persons in search of academic education have traveled from one center of learning to another. It seems worthwhile to introduce the

narrative of this book by reviewing the span of international contacts in higher education. Although a detailed
description of all forms of international education or activities cannot be attempted in one chapter, enough material can be furnished to illustrate the truth that intellectual exchanges and international travels by students and
teachers constitute a viable, important ingredient of higher
education.

These academic linkages and contacts have existed
since earliest times, in vastly different educational institutions, and in widely separated geographical areas. International involvement and commitment are continuous threads
through the history of higher education.

INDIA

On the vast subcontinent of India, student migration
dates to the beginning of higher education there. The early
universities of India, such as the University at Takshasila
(also spelled Taxila, Takkasila),[1] acquired so great a reputation that serious students were willing to make an educational pilgrimage, frequently involving thousands of
miles, to learn, to study, to become scholars, or simply to
discuss important questions of the time. The knowledge
transmitted at this important educational center clearly
transcended provincial barriers.[2] There emerged in India
during that period an academic community of a high level,
attracting by its intellectual weight students and scholars
alike.

From all over India, though not yet from foreign countries, "there was a steady movement of qualified students
drawn from all classes and ranks of society towards Taxila
to complete the education they had [received] in the

schools of their native places."[3] Having their sons, most often barely at the age of sixteen, journey thousands of miles at a time when the difficulties of overland travel can be only imagined, testified to "the great concerns felt by their parents in their proper education."[4]

Taxila itself had developed out of the schools of the gurus and was simply an aggregate of these academies without a central administration.[5] Each teacher had about five hundred students, the tuition was paid in advance, and poor students did menial tasks to earn their keep. After overland travel by foot or on animals—travel that involved physical hardship and often danger as well—the students arrived at Taxila to "round out" their educations. At Taxila they covered a wide variety of courses, such as military science, medicine, and the "Vedas," or Hindu holy books.

Yet not only students journeyed to this most important center of learning in ancient India. Since its fame was due to the fame of its teachers, Taxila also "attracted scholars from different and distant parts of India."[6] Taxila scholars were regarded as "world-renowned" authorities and experts by their students and the general community alike. Of one such teacher we read that young students came "from all India to be taught the arts by him."[7] It was the presence of scholars of such acknowledged authority and widespread reputation that made Taxila the intellectual capital of India. Ultimately, however, this center of learning began to decline, and it had completely disappeared by the first century A.D.

In time Taxila was replaced by the Buddhist University of Nalanda. Again, a highly mobile intellectual community was created, since Nalanda was populated by scholars and students from all parts of the India-Pakistan subcontinent. For the first time, the attraction of an Indian center of learning broadened to include foreign countries; students came from Mongolia, China, Korea, Tibet, and Tocharia. Nalanda, which had grown from Buddhist monastery schools, flourished as an international university for several centuries. In the fifth century it had a population of 8,500 students living in thirteen monasteries. "Nalanda was an international education center . . . when Europe was the darkest watch of the long night of the Middle Ages, when even Saracenic schools and Arabic seats of learning had not yet been founded."[8]

Students who returned to their own countries after several years at Nalanda were looked upon as "scholars" and rewarded with important positions, usually in the governmental bureaucracy of their home country. Such was its reputation that the "highest academic degree of distinction of the times was a Fellowship of Nalanda."[9] The university constituted the "highest court of judges of intellectual worth [and] the stamp of its approval was necessary for any opinion to gain currency in the country."[10] No wonder students traveled from all over Asia to try to gain entrance, which was highly selective. Only about 20 percent of those seeking admission succeeded, and "of those from abroad who wished to enter the Schools of Discussion, the majority, beaten by the difficulties of the problems, withdrew; and [only] those who were deeply versed in old and modern learning were admitted."[11]

Thus, early Indian educational institutions were probably the first providers of an international higher education.[12] The wandering students and scholars who populated these educational establishments provided the model for subsequent learning centers to be established in other countries. The pattern established by these first international universities in India was to continue throughout the history of higher education all over the world. That pattern included young students as well as older scholars. It has to be remembered, though, that life expectancy then was less than half of what it is today, and university study began early. Those who were accepted probably engaged in more serious and disciplined study than most students today. This tradition of earnest study was rewarded by academic maturity in spite of youth.

CHINA

A model similar to that developed in India appeared in China long before the Europeans learned of it. When China was still a feudal state, scholars wandered the countryside teaching and lecturing wherever and whenever they could. One of these scholars, Confucius, taught in various feudal demesnes throughout his life, as did many others.[13] During the Han dynasty (206 B.C.–A.D. 220) an educational system gradually developed that was tightly controlled by the state bureaucracy, with the curriculum centering on the doctrines of Confucius.

Around 100 B.C. higher education became concentrated in the national capital (Chang An).[14] Thus, there developed a pattern of migration by Chinese students, which lasted many centuries. Promising students, recommended by regional officials, traveled to the capital to enter institutions of higher learning there, with room and board provided by the government.[15] Upon completion of their studies they were supposed to return to their former places of residence; however, not all of them did so, since many graduates preferred to stay in the capital.

Up to that point, student migration in China resembled the Indian precedent in being random and subject merely to the attraction of scholarly centers. To this system there was now added a unique and lasting feature—a centrally imposed examination procedure, which enabled itinerant scholars to become mandarins. As mandarins they enjoyed not only an entitlement to a civil service position but also an exalted intellectual and social rank that set them above most of the population.

The formal examination structure encompassed a series of examinations beginning at the provincial level and leading up to the national level. Scholars and students, as they passed these examination levels, became concentrated in population centers. "From the seventh century onward the effect of the competitive civil service examination system on social mobility became tangible."[16] The three-tier examination structure that ultimately developed established county, provincial, and finally municipal levels of attainment; the last entitled the successful candidate to civil status in the capital. "In addition to being the major avenue to social and political advancement, the examinations served the purpose of preserving the Confucian orthodoxy which in its time justified the social structure."[17]

Chinese institutions of higher learning, originally rather traditional and conservative, became more interested in intellectual cooperation with other countries during the T'ang Dynasty (A.D. 618 to A.D. 907). Most of the rulers of this dynasty encouraged international intellectual cooperation and welcomed religious and cultural ideas from other lands.

In time, Chinese education attracted and began to absorb foreign scholars and students. For example, in A.D. 639 Emperor Tai Tsung founded an institute for instruction in literature and the classics, which was open to foreign students. In 705 Emperor Chung Tsung opened national institutions to foreign students coming from countries bordering China. In addition, Chinese teachers started to venture abroad. During the T'ang Dynasty, the

Chinese traveling scholars Hiuen Tsang and I'Tsing brought back favorable reports about the quality of Indian universities such as Nalanda.[18]

The ultimate in intellectual cooperation and cultural borrowing between Chinese and foreign scholars was Japan's adaptation of Chinese language and culture. During the Nara period, Japanese scholars and students crossed the difficult Straits of Japan to China to study Buddhism, Confucianism, and Chinese language, art, and science.[19] After a long and arduous overland route through country infested with bandits, Japanese scholars reached the Chinese capital, where they sought permission to reside. Some stayed for decades. To this day, Chinese culture is firmly established in Japan. "These scholars, then, these priests, artists and craftsmen brought back to Japan the knowledge and the material objects by which their country was to take over and fashion to her own requirements a superior culture."[20] Japanese calligraphy, religion, and philosophy owe much to the international travels of ancient scholars.

The comprehensive and widespread Chinese educational system attracted quite young scholars who, bound by filial obligation to their families and tutors, applied themselves to study with the great diligence for which China has become famous. One witnesses today the same traditional, conservative, and yet international system of higher education, perpetuated by young students, yet losing none of its scholarship, none of its dynamics, and, indeed, none of its elegance.

PERSIA

The Far Eastern tradition established by India and continued by China was furthered in Persia. The University of Jundishapur (Gundisapur) became the most renowned center of higher learning of the sixth-century world. Its range was unmistakably international. Greek, Syrian, Hindu, Jewish and, possibly, Chinese scholars exchanged and examined scientific and intellectual ideas with the Persians.

The historical sources on Jundishapur provide a vivid picture of a thriving intellectual community. "The town is an ancient one. The hospital, medical schools, and university date back to . . . A.D. 271. The teaching here at first was probably in Sanskrit, and Indian medical methods prevailed."[21] With the number of Greek scholars and philosophers coming to Persia increasing, both Greek and Indian influences entered "into Persian intellectual activities."[22] "Greek philosophers [presumably Neoplatonists] . . . were well received."[23]

The extent of Persian intellectual influence is not known in detail, but "[many] scholars [are] attributing a Persian origin to much of later Islamic science and learning."[24] Jundishapur's impact on the Islamic intellectual world was great; knowledge flowed from Jundishapur to Islamic learning centers in the form of Hindu, Persian, Syrian, and Greek works translated into Arabic.[25] From the sixth century on, "the level of educational attainment under Islam was exceptionally high."[26]

The pattern of international student travel, begun in India and expanded in China and Persia, continued under the Muslims. Young scholars traveled in ever-increasing numbers and to an ever-broadening geographic area. "Talented students who aspired for an advanced education were expected to travel to Damascus, Alexandria and Baghdad to hear the great teachers. Just as the international language of educated men in the Mediterranean had once been Greek, so Arabic [had become] the common language of the scholars who roamed from the Indus to the Atlantic in the pursuit of knowledge."[27] Persian higher education fit the international mold.

In time Jundishapur was supplanted by more advanced centers of learning in Baghdad, Samaria, Cordova, and other Spanish and Sicilian academic communities. One of the most outstanding of these educational centers was Al-Azhar. Founded in A.D. 970, it gained renown early in its history as an international school for Islamic studies. A varied mix of subjects including religion, languages, law, and science were taught to students from a wide variety of countries in the Moslem world.[28] Another outstanding example was the Karawain University (Madrassah) in Fez, Morocco, which together with other ancient centers of Muslim higher education in North Africa attracted increasingly large numbers of itinerant students from all over the region.

GREECE

Western educational tradition began with the unfolding of Hellenic culture. Greece quickly assumed a dominant position with an early educational system in which the Sophist method of instruction became the accepted mode. In his dialogues *Protagoras* and *Theages,* Plato describes the throngs of Greek and foreign students who followed these "pied pipers of learning" from city to city to satiate their intellectual curiosity. The scholars charged rather high fees for their services as they moved about the country. "Many affluent foreign students followed the Sophists in their travels and learned from them how to become statesmen in their home countries or Sophist teachers themselves."[29] One of the main contributions these wandering scholars made was their emphasis on the human body, while still considering the teaching of the mind to be of primary importance.[30]

Protagoras, perhaps the most famous of the Sophists, was himself a foreigner. He started teaching near his home town of Abdera and gradually made his way to Athens, where he ended up as one of Pericles' advisers. Even in his later years, he was absent from Athens for long periods of time.[31] Whether in Athens or traveling around the country, Protagoras always had a group of disciples with him, some native-born and some foreign students.[32]

The intellectual prowess of the Sophists, to which the brilliance of their antagonist Socrates added a powerful stimulus, filled the philosophy and rhetoric schools of Athens with students from all quarters of the world.[33] "And so men came to think of her as the University of higher culture, in which were represented all the studies of the age. . . . Soon, indeed, Athens . . . became the school not only of Greece, but the world . . . and in the third and fourth centuries she was, beyond compare, the foremost of the Universities then known."[34]

When Plato set up his Academy in Athens he established the first permanent institution of higher education in Greece.[35] Within a short period of time other teachers, such as Isocrates, the rhetorician, established their own schools, and the importance of the wandering scholars, though not of students, started to decline.

About fifty years later, Aristotle, the respected tutor of Alexander the Great, settled into the Lyceum as a teacher. By that time the various Athenian schools, small in number in the beginning, started to fight over students. Rich foreign students were especially welcomed by some of these institutions, and they came to Athens from wherever the Greek language was spoken, including Asia Minor.[36]

"As they came at . . . an early age from distant homes, and their parents very rarely could be with them . . . they often had their personal attendants . . . or private tutors, to exercise some control, and represent the influence of home."[37] These attendants were usually servants of lower social rank and, therefore, could exert only minimal control over their charges. It was up to the lecturers to "speak of themselves as shepherds and their audience as a flock which they must lead."[38]

Athens became a city of increasing international flavor, as the students from different nations exhibited their pronounced national differences in behavior. We read of these differences being "so strongly marked as if they had some organized form of clubs or social unions among them, somewhat as in later days we read in modern Universities of standing jealousies between north and south, or recognized subdivisions into nations. There are some data even which may lead us to infer that not only were the students to be distinguished as *gownsmen* from the world, but that each nation had its own variety of academic garb."[39]

After Macedonia took over Athens, the two largest schools—the Academy and the Lyceum—were combined to form the University of Athens. Thus, as Athens lost political importance it gained even more prestige as an intellectual center of the Western world. As a result, the number of foreign students increased further.[40]

The only possible rival to Athens in academic prestige at this time was the Museum at Alexandria. Its establishment was perhaps the greatest contribution of Greek higher education to world knowledge. "The institution at Alexandria was made up of a collection of research institutes to which scholars came from all over the Hellenistic world to pursue their studies and to which younger men came to work as disciples of the older masters. A definite corporate and community life grew up around common meeting and dining rooms, attractive promenades, and an extraordinary library. . . . It was in a sense the forerunner of the 'think tank' where scholars gathered to advance knowledge or to synthesize it."[41]

ROME

Higher education during Roman times was based to such a degree on the Greek model that it has been labeled "an imitation of Greece."[42] The Romans were the first to use a foreign language (Greek) to increase mastery over their own language[43] and to become bilingual.[44]

Most Roman rulers strongly encouraged exchanges with foreign academicians and scholars.[45] Thus, Greek scholars started to appear in Rome in ever-increasing numbers. Such intellectual contacts "opened the way for the young Romans to enjoy a more extended period of study abroad."[46] It often happened that

Romans with intellectual interests, when on official service abroad, would take the opportunity of visiting one or other of the main centres of learning, in order to listen to their leading scholars, and perhaps to join in friendly discussion with them. Athens, Rhodes and various cities of Asia Minor welcomed such visits, which could give rise to a stimulating exchange of ideas, and sometimes led to an invitation to join a Roman retinue or to teach in Rome. Athens and the philosophical lectures and discussions of a flourishing New Academy proved a particular attraction.[47]

One example of a young traveling scholar in search of the best education possible was the great Roman poet

Virgil. He was born and first went to school in Andes, a small village and a dependency of the city of Mantua.

> When he was twelve, he went to the grammarian in Cremona. At fifteen or sixteen . . . he went to Milan to learn rhetoric, then went to Rome, to study under the famous rhetor M. Epidius. . . . The future poet, whose interests were very wide, also studied the sciences—medicine and above all mathematics. This led him on to philosophy, and . . . he was converted to the Epicurism that the Roman intellectuals of the time found so congenial . . . ; he then went to Naples and joined the philosopher Siro's school and became a member of the Epicurean circle that centered round Philodemus in Herculaneum.[48]

Like most Roman students, Virgil started his itinerant education at the early age of twelve, and by the time he had completed his scholarly pursuits he had traveled to most of the intellectual centers of the Roman world.

The educational facilities in the Roman Empire varied substantially from locality to locality. It is "fairly easy to pick out the great university centers, where there was a relatively high number of famous teachers who drew large numbers of students, sometimes from a great distance—and fought as fiercely over them as their Greek colleagues in the East."[49]

In Italy proper, these main centers were to be found in Naples and Milan, where their prestige was enhanced "by the fact that the Imperial court of the West was there. But of course for Italy and the whole of the Latin Empire the great university centre was Rome, which was far more important than any of the others."[50] Thus,

> to Rome came all the most famous grammarians and rhetors, both Latin and Greek . . . [and] the emperor

did all he could to entice them and keep them there. Rome was perhaps the only place in the West where there was any organized teaching of philosophy, and, most important of all, where there was an official centre for the teaching of law. Law was in great demand, and great numbers of students came to Rome from the provinces—not only from all parts of Italy, but from Africa, Gaul, the Danubian provinces and even from the Greek lands in the east.[51]

The pattern of international exposure for young itinerant students was now firmly established in the Western world.

The main contribution of the Romans to the field of international education rested in their increased emphasis upon the exchange of international scholars and their recognition of the values present in other cultures,[52] particularly the Greek system of thought. They recognized that the training of citizens for a Roman world order was a most desirable end of the educational process in itself.

WESTERN EUROPE

The Greek and Roman tradition of international exchange in higher education survived the Dark Ages with some modifications. Medieval universities in Europe, with few exceptions, received legitimization from a charter granted by the kings or popes, which usually assured the perpetuation of the particular institution.

From the beginning these centers of learning rested on itinerant students and scholars. "All the universities of the 13th Century were international."[53] Taken together, "they constituted an intellectual common world, embodying the same ideal, fulfilling the same function, exchanging teachers, students and ideas."[54]

The mutual exchange of knowledge, furthered by the existence of a common language (Latin) and the large degree of mobility of students and teachers, was a prime promoter of internationalism. Through this mode of knowledge transmission, the organizational structure, subject content, and teaching methods of noteworthy universities such as Bologna and Paris were in time introduced to other countries. The medieval university started to internationalize learning to an extent that had not been realized previously. Furthermore, scholars were awarded special privileges, rights, and immunities.[55] For the first time, a university, the University of Paris, could justifiably be called a "world university."[56] These well-known and highly respected institutions of higher learning in Western Europe, however, were preceded by two phenomena, the "cathedral schools" and the "wandering scholars."

Even though specific goals had been prescribed for the church schools, "their size and qualifications varied widely, not only from country to country, but from city to city."[57] More importantly, they differed in terms of staying power, a matter related to patronage. It was patronage, the teaching of a new field, a new method of inquiry, a famous teacher, or most importantly "the attitude (progressive or conservative) of bishop and canons, [which] could make the difference between growth and stagnation, fame and obscurity. But whether a school achieved success or failure, its efforts added to the atmosphere of learning that marked the twelfth century and ultimately helped the early universities to sink roots and grow."[58]

These isolated cathedral schools could not have been welded into the world of higher education without the ever-increasing network of communication provided by students and scholars traveling from place to place, exchanging ideas and services. Thus, it is essentially the "wandering scholar" who made it possible for some of the better known cathedral schools to expand into universities, and it was "the comparative ease with which a student could travel that, in turn, made these traveling scholars possible."[59] Both itinerant students and scholars were a prominent feature of the intellectual climate of the times.

> Except for the physical and technical handicaps that impeded travel in general at that period, [the scholar] encountered few obstacles when moving from one place to another. For all purposes of culture, political boundaries between nations were immaterial. News, ideas, and books travelled faster than is generally assumed. To those who travelled for the sake of learning . . . the roads were open from one end of the former Carolingian Empire to the other. Also, since Christian learning was of universal scope, it was thought of as being epitomized in a Studium as universal as Empire and Church. A scholar might well be aware of differences separating him from a fellow student in other regions; still he might have been constantly reminded that they had a common heritage: the Latin language, the Latin literature both sacred and profane. . . . When setting out . . . to venture on the unstable life of an "exile," the scholar was at least sure of finding admittance at any church or school. . . . Local authorities might expel him because of evil deeds and a loose life or because of the spreading of novel ideas, but not on account of his birth or origin. Nobody asked for his papers or bothered him with bureaucratic restrictions or scholastic requirements.[60]

Consolidation of the cathedral schools set the stage for the development of the universities. The centers of learning that developed in places such as Salerno, Bologna, Perugia, Siena, and Paris enjoyed the benefit of a common language. Prior to the Reformation, "every educated man in Western and Central Europe spoke Latin."[61] It was the common language, perhaps more than any other phenomenon, that precipitated the internationalization of the universities.

The University of Paris had become an international institution of higher learning to such an extent that the Faculty of Arts was divided into "nations" according to the various regions of Europe. "Every student entering had to be enrolled in one of the several nations according to the land of his birth. If he came from some region not specifically named in the existent nations then he had to go into the nation whose territory was closest to that of his homeland."[62]

Internationalism was reflected not only in the student body but also in the teaching staff. The English-German "nation" at the University of Paris was second in size to the French "nation" itself,[63] but it is interesting to note that at "the height of its fame not one great teacher of French origin was to be found on the faculties of the University of Paris."[64]

Under Henry II, England recalled many English scholars from Paris as the king strove to sever relations with his enemy, Thomas à Becket; many others were expelled by France during this period. These scholars settled at Oxford and established the first British university.[65] However, Oxford did not long enjoy the privilege of having the only "studium generale" in England.[66] Following a conflict between the university and the townspeople of Oxford, most of the students left, with many settling in Cambridge, "which owes its existence as a university to that immigration."[67]

Gradually, the numbers of foreign scholars at the University of Paris started to decline, especially in the fourteenth and fifteenth centuries. The influence of the University started to recede, but this fact by no means hindered the growth of internationalism in education. Two reasons for the continued growth of internationalism can be cited.

The first was the rapid increase in the number of universities all over Europe.[68] These universities were founded "through a desire on the part of reigning monarchs and princes to glorify themselves and their land by their patronage of learning and the erection of universities, so that their countrymen might not be obliged to seek foreign lands in pursuit of learning."[69] Some of the universities and their founding dates between the fourteenth and sixteenth centuries include:[70]

Pisa, 1343	Tübingen, 1477
Prague, 1348	Copenhagen, 1479
Cracow, 1364	Marburg, 1527
Vienna, 1365	Messina, 1548
Heidelberg, 1386	Jena, 1558
Leipzig, 1409	Leiden, 1575
Louvain, 1425	Graz, 1586
Genoa, 1471	

The second reason was the way in which most of these emerging universities were financed. These institutions were financially secure, supported largely by the monarchs and princes, and less by students' tuition. This fact afforded greater freedom of choice for students and led to increased student migration. The student was now able

to attend the lectures of his choice and even to migrate in the course of his studies from one university to another. This was only possible since there was no fixed syllabus in the majority of subjects. . . . This freedom was even unhampered by anything resembling a tutorial system. The virtues claimed for this arrangement were that it developed a sense of intellectual initiative and responsibility in the student, and that it enabled him to study under the most expert teachers in his particular subjects, irrespective of the university at which they worked.[71]

Desiderius Erasmus (1467–1536), one of the great leaders in humanistic education, can serve as a prime example of the itinerant student/scholar of the time. As a very young child and

while still a pupil at Deventer [he] exhibited remarkable ability in the new learning, and when he was only eight his greatness is said to have been prophesied by Agricola while on a visit to Hegius. After leaving Deventer, Erasmus furthered his knowledge of Latin and Greek at the College de Montaigu at Paris where in 1499 he met a number of English students, and was by them induced to visit Oxford. Here he became acquainted with Colet and More, and studied under Grocyn and Linacre. . . . Yet Erasmus could not help sighing for the Mecca of all devoted humanists, and, after struggling with poverty in the North for seven years, he at length found it possible to visit the ancient Libraries, meet the learned men, and pursue the study of Greek at Venice, Florence, Padua, Bologna, and Rome. In 1510, he returned to England, and for four years occupied the chair of divinity at Cambridge. During this period he also lectured gratuitously upon Greek, and afforded Colet much help in establishing his school at St. Paul's. Three years later he undertook the project of a new humanistic college at Louvain, but in 1422, when the Reformation controversies began, he retired to Basel. In this home . . . he found time to edit, translate, and produce works of his own until his death. Thus Erasmus travelled widely, met all the prominent scholars of his day, and made great contributions to humanism and social reform.[72]

Thus, through the general acceptance of "Lernfreiheit," international travel by university students became a familiar pattern which has survived up to the present. One theme, however, deserves particular attention. During most of the Middle Ages, university students were very young by today's standards. These universities are often regarded as an extension of senior secondary schools, because the granting of the "Licencia docendi" was accomplished sometimes as early as fourteen years of age.[73]

As time passed, the age level of students slowly increased, but the legal and pedagogical notion of students as being in "status pupilari" remains. This notion can be traced to the historical practice of compulsory attendance at lectures and examinations and the authoritarian control of tutors over students, reminding one of the stance of a grammar-school master.

Historically, then, the universities of Europe carried on the tradition of "universitas," of world rather than national organization, and, at least originally, of catering to very young students. While this feature of university life continued somewhat undisturbed, two new elements were added to further enrich life in the academy. The first was the appearance in the seventeenth century of scientific organizations, which deregionalized, one might say, separatist tendencies in favor of maintaining an international intellectual community. The second, equally significant, was the emergence in Europe of one nation that quickly assumed the former role of Paris. Germany, through the establishment of a cohesive and successful educational system, became the focus of academic migration.

More and more, academicians in newly emerging disciplines joined together to create scientific associations. These associations appeared with increasing frequency in the seventeenth century. The Berlin Academy of Science, the Academy of Science in Paris, and the Royal Society of London all were formed during this period.[74] These learned societies initiated global intellectual cooperation through correspondence, teacher exchanges or visits to foreign countries, attendance at international conferences, and translation of scientific material into other languages. International cooperation was soon firmly established in the academic community. Scholars increasingly crossed frontiers, and books and articles were exchanged and circulated extensively. In scientific research, teams in different countries became interdependent and began to build upon one another.

Finally, in the nineteenth century Germany became "the Mecca of foreign students, above all of Americans from the United States."[75] Scholars and students from all over the world studied at German universities. Thus, one more chapter in the long history of academic migration was written. For a brief report on the German university at that time we can turn to the eminent British scientist, T. H. Huxley:[76]

It is not thus that the German universities, from being beneath notice a century ago, have become what they now are—the most intensely cultivated and the most productive intellectual corporations the world has ever seen.

The student who repairs to them sees in the list of classes and of professors a fair picture of the world of knowledge. Whatever he needs to know there is some one ready to teach him, some one competent to discipline him in the way of learning; whatever his special bent, let him but be able and diligent, and in due time he shall find distinction and a career. Among his professors, he sees men whose names are known and revered throughout the civilized world; and their living example infects him with a noble ambition, and a love for the spirit of work.

In short, in Germany, the universities are exactly what the Rector of Lincoln and the Commissioners tell us the English universities are not; that is to say, corporations "of learned men devoting their lives to the cultivation of science, and the direction of academical education." They are not "boarding schools for youths," nor clerical seminaries; but institutions for the higher culture of men, in which the theological faculty is of no more importance, or prominence, than the rest; and which are truly "universities," since they strive to represent and embody the totality of human knowledge, and to find room for all forms of intellectual activity.[77]

Huxley sums up his vivid description by stating that, "although one does not find England's greatest thinkers in university halls, the case is just the reverse in Germany."[78] It was for that reason that "between 1815 and 1914, more than 10,000 young Americans were enrolled in German institutions of higher learning. . . . The 'vision of excellence across the seas' resulted in a 'transatlantic scholarly migration,' one of the most extraordinary examples of cultural interaction in the history of higher education."[79] To look at the centers of learning in Western Europe, from the cathedral schools in early medieval times to the great universities in the nineteenth century, to study academic life, from the wandering scholars to the student invasion of Germany prior to 1914, is to realize that institutions of higher education as we know them today would not exist without this constant intercultural cross-fertilization and the unending exchange of new ideas and intellectual values.

CONCLUSIONS

World Wars I and II have come and gone. In their wake has arrived a new age of international exchanges of ideas in education, which is summarized here in bare outline.

The two wars, for better or worse, stimulated international contacts, narrowing the gap not only between Europe and the United States, but also between Western countries and the Orient and, indeed, the rest of the world. A great variety of new and exciting modes of communication, not the least by satellites in space, have stimulated international contacts and cross-cultural exposure. Through television and other forms of visual representation nations can be brought closer to one another.

In adult education there has been a burgeoning of enrichment of (1) information and (2) persons. First, library materials—writings from abroad, in the original and in translation, and foreign newspapers and magazines are available not only in more countries but also in more remote areas within countries. Second, international conferences of scholars, reciprocal visits of faculty, national scientific missions abroad, and technical development projects have greatly expanded adult academic contacts.

The League of Nations and later the United Nations have influenced the international cultural community both directly and indirectly. On university campuses one notices faculty development in international and area studies, foreign-language libraries, research concentrated abroad, and a general internationalization of curricula. The creation of schools of international affairs and area institutes within universities has further contributed to a general decrease of isolationalism and ethnocentrism. Institutions such as the University of the United Nations in Tokyo,[80] the College of Europe in Bruges, and the University of Europe in Florence are in the vanguard of international learning. Other organizations, for example the Institute of International Education (IIE) or the Council on International Education Exchange (CIEE), organize and administer a variety of programs and services in the field of international educational exchange. Supranational agencies such as UNESCO and UNITAR have been working and doing research in the international field for more than three decades.

For the student age group, the ever-increasing number of Junior Year Abroad programs registered is an established feature of international educational exchange. In addition, there are many government-sponsored programs, such as the well-known Fulbright scholarship program in the United States, which finance students and scholars abroad. Many governments, such as those of newly independent African countries like Nigeria and Kenya, sponsor their students abroad on a large scale.

In addition to those taking part in official programs, the number of individual students in foreign institutions has increased steadily, frequently doubling in less than a decade. The result has been a virtual flood of foreign students on American campuses, while in some countries institutions such as the Patrice Lumumba University of Friendship of the Peoples in Moscow or the International Christian University in Tokyo were established specifically to accommodate foreign students. It is difficult indeed to think of colleges or universities in any country not affected by applicants from abroad seeking admission to courses of study.

Even the secondary-school age group is gaining increasing exposure to different cultures. The Boy Scouts International, the American Field Service, the Czech Sokol, the GAPP (German-American Partnership Program), and the American-Scandinavian Exchange Program are only some of the many organizations sponsoring overseas travel or exchange programs for the below-college age group. Through summer camps abroad, pen-pal programs, individual family travel, and in many other uncharted ways, more and more school-age children are being introduced to foreign countries. The sophistication of secondary- and even primary-school programs to internationalize their textbooks, to teach world history, or to offer bilingual or intensive language programs are only symptoms of this great change, a description of which is clearly outside the scope of this book.

One matter remains bewildering. While the very young of precollege age and the junior, senior, and graduate college-age groups are afforded international exposure and cross-cultural contacts, nothing of substance has been done to provide international experiences for the freshman and sophomore college student.

2. Community Colleges and Overseas Academic Programs

The previous chapter illustrated the prominence of an international component in the creation of institutions of higher learning. The roles of the wandering scholar and itinerant student were shown to be important throughout the history of education. The focus of the book will shift now to a discussion of the rationale for the involvement in international programs of one of the youngest institutions in higher education.

The concept of introducing a sizable international dimension into the community college was an almost radical idea when it was tried for the first time. Most previous attempts had failed in the planning stages, largely because of a number of erroneous assumptions and misconceptions. A discussion of these misconceptions will reveal their spurious basis and will lead to the reasons for introducing international programs into community colleges. The chapter will provide a number of arguments in favor of the question.

ARGUMENT 1

One widely held assumption states that students should have at least two years of college training, or perhaps a two-year waiting period, prior to studying abroad. It is argued that students can benefit from overseas academic programs only after they have been in college for at least two years and, therefore, that overseas academic programs should be reserved for undergraduate juniors or seniors and graduate students. It is thought that their institutions are better equipped to introduce these students to overseas academic experiences during their first two years on campus. Only after this introductory experience, the argument goes, is the student supposed to have reached the proper degree of maturity and academic training.

While it is difficult to understand today why a student could not benefit from exposure to a foreign culture unless he had spent two years in an institution of higher learning, one can see, perhaps, that when the Junior Year Abroad program was started[1] mass education of American youth had not yet become a reality. At that time America was still educating the "elite," and the idea that a semester or a year abroad would contribute to the well-rounded education of a young person was fashionable. Furthermore, the argument continued, the junior year might be the best possible point in a student's intellectual maturity to ship him overseas for the added cultural exposure. At this time the student was thought not to be set in his ways and, therefore, receptive enough to benefit from whatever Europe had to offer. Furthermore, the junior year perhaps best fit into the curriculum structure of a four-year college, in that the third year seemed to be the most logical time during the four-year program for a student to be away from his campus.

These arguments were developed with some justification for a particular student population. Yet, as American education gradually changed from education of the elite to mass higher education, the arguments for the Junior Year Abroad program became redundant. The third year was the best possible time for students to study overseas because this is the way it had always been.

In an age of instant communication and jet travel, two years of college education are no longer essential to introduce a student to another culture or a different educational system. Public sophistication is on the rise, and television has undertaken serious educational efforts such as the "Open University" in England, the "Sunrise Semester" in the United States, and the "Television University" in Japan. Young people are exposed to other cultures by the various media to a far greater degree than were college students prior to World War II. In addition, many more students entering college today have already traveled abroad.

Thus, the idea that a student must spend his freshman and sophomore year on an American campus before going overseas simply is no longer valid. Furthermore, early exposure to a foreign culture or a different educational system can be an advantage in college. It has been shown that early travel to other countries and exposure to foreign cultures is of substantial benefit to students. Students who have been abroad for a semester prior to their junior year frequently become seriously interested in a geographical area, country, religion, or philosophy and pursue their interest upon their return to this country. Had they traveled abroad only as juniors, perhaps not enough time would have been left in their four-year academic programs for them to undertake seriously the study of their new interest.

Thus, if one accepts the argument that the junior year abroad concept was narrow from the start and was developed for a time when the students were different and when instant communication and jet travel had not yet become a way of life, one has to conclude that freshmen and sophomores cannot be excluded any longer from the vital educational experience of introduction to other cultures and other educational systems.

ARGUMENT 2

A second question is raised by the well-known two-year discrepancy between European and American high-school graduates. Most European universities do not allow American students to enter directly out of high school. They require American students to complete about two years of college studies in the United States prior to acceptance into their first-year programs. The reason for this policy is simple. European high-school graduates have stayed in school one to two years longer than their American counterparts, and they have usually covered more subjects in greater depth. Therefore, they can begin their university studies in a single subject and do not have to spend the first two years in a "studium generale."

By the same token, graduates of most European high schools, upon entering an American college or university, will receive anywhere from one to two years of college credit, owing to their advanced secondary training. The German student with the "Abitur," the French student with the "Baccalaureat" or the British student with his "A levels" is better prepared to start his university studies than the American student fresh out of high school. These comparisons hold equally well for students from Russia, Japan, or most other industrialized countries.

If it is impossible, the argument goes, for the American freshman or sophomore to be channeled directly into a European university, why not provide him with two years of college studies in this country before sending him abroad during his third year? Perhaps the junior year abroad was correct after all!

However, if a student should not be sent abroad unless qualified to enter a specific educational institution, the argument is no longer whether the student is prepared to experience a foreign culture or benefit from being exposed to a foreign environment but whether or not he is qualified to enter a specific foreign university. The emphasis is thus shifted from the benefits the American student might receive through an experience abroad to the academic characteristics of the foreign institutions. From a technical point of view, it is indeed virtually impossible to channel community-college students directly into European universities. The solution to this problem is twofold: (1) establishing of overseas academic programs geared specifically to the American freshman or sophomore; and (2) bypassing the institutions traditionally involved in Junior Year Abroad programs and searching out others on the academic level of community colleges. This dual solution allows for flexibility and creativity the students can utilize. The selection process for colleges overseas that can administer academic programs may lead to the development of new and exciting programs. Innovative programs, such as community-based or work-study projects, may also be created.

The community-college movement is a recent, vibrant, innovative, and dynamic educational subsystem, and it follows that this dynamism and innovation should be applied to the development of overseas programs for community college students.

In conclusion, it can be noted that the community-college movement in this country has been paralleled in various ways in other countries. The community-college movement in the United States led directly to the development of similar institutions in some countries, while other countries have developed similar institutions on their own.

If freshmen and sophomores are to participate in meaningful academic programs abroad, then educational institutions that are able to administer these programs should be located and utilized. It cannot be left to the foreign institution to accept or reject American college students. Innovative and dynamic educators in this country can help develop new programs or single out new institutions overseas that can provide viable academic programs for American freshmen and sophomores.

ARGUMENT 3

The supposed necessity to speak another language is another argument by which American lower-division students have been excluded from overseas study. There are several ways to assess this situation: First, while it is correct that most community-college students do not have the facility to converse in a foreign language or the ability to follow a lecture in a foreign institution in a language not their own, it is equally true that most American juniors also lack the ability to follow university lectures in a foreign language. Many Junior Year Abroad programs today are being taught in English.

It is fervently hoped that all American students overseas, whether they be freshmen, sophomores, juniors or seniors, study the language of their host country while abroad. However, fluency in a foreign language should not be the determining factor for the participation of a student in an overseas academic program.

Second, it is frequently not a matter of speaking the foreign language per se. There are some excellent overseas academic programs in small countries where it simply does not pay for a student to engage in any extensive study of the language before going abroad. For example, one can cite the case of Denmark. There are only about four million persons today who speak Danish (less than one-third the population of Tokyo), and the majority of Danes are able to converse in English. Yet there are excellent overseas academic programs for American students in that country. Unless a student intends to specialize in the Danish language or wants to work and live in that country after graduation, it would be difficult to justify an intensive study of Danish prior to spending a semester in that country. The excellent study program being conducted in English by Danish instructors at the University of Copenhagen through the study division of the Danmarks Internationale Studenterkomite (DIS) provides a perfect solution. While the student is encouraged to take a course in Danish while living in Denmark, he is introduced to a foreign culture and, at the same time, participates in a first-rate academic program, with the courses taught in English.

Third, there are obviously foreign countries where English is the spoken language (Australia, England, Ireland). Therefore, it is indeed possible to provide American college students with overseas academic programs in several foreign cultures where the absence of foreign-language facility does not constitute a problem.

Fourth, experience has shown that some students have started to study a foreign language after their return from a short-term introductory program abroad. Rather than waiting until a student has mastered a foreign language, a program overseas introduces the student to another language, thereby demonstrating to him the fact that a second language can provide him with an added perspective. Thus, he may want to start serious language studies after his return. To delay sending students overseas until they speak a foreign language would deny a vast segment of the American college-age population a meaningful academic experience in another country. American students in general are extremely reluctant to study a foreign language.[2] Therefore, any means by which American students will be introduced to that process and encouraged to pursue it can only benefit them at a time when economic interdependency requires greater facility with foreign languages in any industrialized country.

Fifth, many American youngsters are going abroad on visits, travels, or even for extended periods, living in a foreign culture without making any attempt to familiarize themselves with the language, much less engaging in a serious effort to study the language while abroad. A solid overseas academic experience can introduce the American freshman or sophomore to a foreign language through the imposition of a formal, structured educational program. The choice of studying or not studying the language may no longer be the student's. Many a college student has found that his academic experience in a foreign country is vastly enriched through the added requirement of participation in a formal language program while overseas. As stated above, most American study programs overseas now require students to take at least one course in the local language.

ARGUMENT 4

Another debate, essentially philosophical in nature, revolves around the idea that community colleges are predominantly designed as institutions to serve the immediate community.

"The community college is rooted in the soil of the community it serves. It draws its strength from that community. It gives to that community the learning that man has accumulated, the arts and sciences that are our greatest weapons in the perpetual war against poverty of the mind and the body. The community sustains the college and the college enriches the community."[3] Many community-college catalogs start out with words similar to this statement that proclaim, in effect, the commitment the college has to the immediate community. Since it is the county that pays part of the operating expenses of the institutions, it is felt strongly that the immediate community should be the chief beneficiary of the colleges. "To the college come the youth of the community, the intellectually gifted and those who find learning difficult: those who wish to study to prepare for careers in business, industry and health services."[4] The rationale and the administrative potential of overseas academic programs at the community-college level thus is put into question. While it is true that these institutions are planned to enrich and assist the local community, a closer appraisal of this statement is necessary.

It is difficult to understand why the statements cited above should automatically imply any emphasis on regionalism and the immediate area to the exclusion of internationalism and a concern for global awareness. With the world becoming increasingly interdependent, no college can fulfill its function of educating today's student without a sizable international dimension. An international commitment has to be part of the mission to educate young people for the twenty-first century.[5]

If exposure to a different culture is beneficial to third-year college students participating in overseas academic programs, such exposure should be just as beneficial, or perhaps more so, to freshmen and sophomores. Community colleges, closely linked to the immediate community, need the experiences and modus operandi of a structured international dimension. Only then can they fulfill their function of educating the citizens of the state. A commitment to international exposure through structured and comprehensive academic programs overseas must be part of that dimension.

ARGUMENT 5

In addition to the function of educating their students for the century ahead, it seems reasonable to expect that colleges would also wish to enhance their own position. Another reason community colleges would want to introduce international programs would be to portray themselves as striving for enhanced academic prestige.

The creation, rapid development, and mushrooming of community colleges in the United States has resulted in a number of problems not originally anticipated. One is the purpose for which these institutions were set up in the first place. "Every major explosion of numbers in the history of higher education has brought forth new institutions described and describing themselves as mass academies. Some of these perished; others were in time converted to institutions of high status."[6] It was, and still is, exactly the striving for higher status that has frequently put pressure on community colleges and caused them to emulate the more advanced colleges in mounting international programs.

Within the framework of community colleges a tremendous variety of institutions has developed with a vast diversity in emphasis, content, quality, orientation, and commitment. "This diversity of program and purpose is one of the most valuable assets of the community junior college; at the same time it increases the difficulty of fitting the institution neatly into the earlier pattern of higher education."[7] Yet, "in spite of the problems, stress and strain, and the diversity (or perhaps because of the latter) it can be stated that the community junior college has successfully traversed the trials of infancy and adolescence."[8]

Amid all these aspirations, the idea of international training and overseas educational programming was formed and developed on the community-college level. It is only natural that these colleges, like all new institutions in higher education, would try to upgrade their own standing and attempt to secure the position they occupy within that spectrum. Moreover, they may want to achieve a status reserved for institutions either more advanced, with a greater tradition and history, or already accepted by the community at large. A solid commitment to internationalism is one of the avenues open to these new colleges in their attempt to emulate older and more advanced institutions.

However, the international dimension and strong commitment to international education should be more than an emulation of other institutions. The kind of education any institution provides can be significantly enhanced through the adoption of an international component. The incorporation of such an international commitment on the part of established institutions has never resulted in a lowering of academic standards—on the contrary. The introduction of international dimensions into a community-college setting, therefore, becomes not a matter of prestige or prestige only but a matter of standards—in short, a serious humanistic endeavor. No community college can afford to be without an international commitment if it seriously wants to fulfill its function and be part of the spectrum of institutions of higher learning in today's world.

ARGUMENT 6

Community colleges, as institutions of higher learning, have a responsibility constantly to upgrade the curriculum they offer to their students. Faculty members are necessarily involved in curriculum change. But, "the pressure of non-university faculty to acquire recognition through university status is a basic part of the story of higher education today."[9] Through international education, faculty members in community colleges can be provided with a means to gain the recognition they desire. In all modern societies, international recognition is a higher mark of status than national recognition, and the dedicated involvement of faculty members in overseas academic programs usually leads to a more serious involvement in other global activities. These activities in turn expand the thinking of faculty members beyond the provincial concerns of their own college and community. The excitement of travel and the discovery of foreign cultures, as well as new contacts with colleagues in overseas institutions, provides for added prestige and enhanced social recognition for faculty members.

International education can enrich the faculty in a second way. Every subject taught is a compilation of material from different sources. Contemporary geology, for example, is enriched and supported by historical geology and, at the same time, by advances made in chemistry. Constant interchange among faculty members in different countries enriches not only the faculty but, through them, their institutions. American community colleges may receive support and cooperation from their sister institutions overseas in the development of new and innovative programs. Academic curricula vary from country to country. For example, journalism is not an academic subject in Israel, and criminal justice is not taught in universities in England. On the other hand, dental technologists from the United States could benefit from visits to countries where dental technology has long been taught as an academic subject; they would witness advances in the field that could then be used to improve their colleges' own programs in dental technology. Thus, overseas academic programs will benefit not only community-college students but also the faculty and the institutions themselves.

ARGUMENT 7

Just as faculty members in community colleges may strive for higher status, so do students. It is pointed out that, frequently, students in community colleges "seriously question the justice of being assigned to an inferior station."[10] Thus, demands for academic programs in community colleges increase, including the desire for international involvement.

International programs can provide an excellent mechanism to counteract the extremely high attrition rate in United States colleges during the first two years. Although it is difficult to send freshmen overseas in their first semester, the prospect of participation in a second- or third-semester program abroad may motivate them to stay in school.

However, a much more important argument can be advanced here. For many community-college students, the two-year program will be their only exposure to higher education. It would be grievous, indeed, to deny them their only opportunity to participate in an academically sound and culturally rewarding program overseas. To reserve such a privilege for four-year college students is to deny two-year students the right of equal access to an important aspect of higher education. In addition, since adults in many communities are increasingly turning to the local college as the center of their own learning activities, a sizable international dimension in the college will constitute a valuable enrichment for them. It is a chain reaction: Enrollment in overseas programs by children and younger siblings of adult students and alumni will increase the interest of the entire community in the activities of the community college. The excitement thus generated will serve to increase enrollment, creating more interest, and so on.

Thus, increased attendance at international events sponsored locally by the college, increased media coverage of such events, greater tolerance of minorities and other cultures in the community, increased adult travel abroad, contact between host families following visits abroad, and increased numbers of foreign faculty on campus are just some of the benefits that can accrue to the community college that has an international program.

ARGUMENT 8

A number of questions remain. If an international dimension in the community college is deemed beneficial to the student population and to the college as a whole, the types of programs and the location for these programs have to be discussed.

Countries can be classified into four categories ranging from "very similar" at one extreme to "very different" at the other, with "similar" and "different" in between. For example, the United Kingdom would be "very similar," since the community-college student would not experience any significant language difficulties and many traditions and behavior patterns are, indeed, very similar to those in this country.

For a "similar" country one might look to Italy or France, where English is not spoken and where the culture of the country is dissimilar to some extent.

As a "different" society one could name Japan, where the language is vastly different and where the culture appears strange to most Americans, although the country is industrialized and shares some common denominators with this country.

In the fourth category one would list underdeveloped or Third World countries, where living conditions can be difficult and the culture would appear "very different" to most American college freshmen or sophomores.

While a good argument can be made for an overseas academic program in a "different" or even a "very different" society, so as to provide a student with an experience totally unlike his own, one must remember that the majority of these students have never before been outside the United States; indeed, many have never traveled beyond their own immediate region. To some, a trip to a large city might qualify as a trip to a "very different" environment.

In addition, there is a substantial difference in sophistication and maturity between sophomores and graduate or postdoctoral students. The motivation of the student also must be taken into account. While a graduate student working on a very specialized art-history project might be willing to endure very difficult living conditions so as to be able to study the cave paintings of Ajanta in India, one cannot expect the same willingness on the part of a college sophomore who wants to spend a semester in a foreign country.

Two additional arguments present themselves: Many parents would want their children to spend a semester abroad during their college career. Since the parents often are providing the economic means for the semester abroad, they are in a position to influence the choice of location for the overseas academic experience. Most parents would want their children to study in a society from which the family has emigrated to the United States or with which the family maintains ties. Even if families are not recent émigrés, many want their children to study in Europe, hence, the Eurocentric character of most overseas academic programs attached to institutions of higher learning in this country.

If we add the fact that air fare to Europe is approximately half that to Africa or the Far East, one can easily understand that the pressure on the colleges for the establishment of programs in Europe is, indeed, significant. It would seem that community colleges in particular would have to respond to these pressures, exerted as they are by the parents, who are paying for the students' experiences abroad. For these reasons the vast majority of programs for community colleges overseas will be in countries that are "very similar" or "similar" to the United States.

ARGUMENT 9

In conclusion, we can mention several additional arguments for the introduction of overseas academic programs into community colleges that can be used to support those listed above.

A paper from the State University of New York, Office of International Programs, states that:

> International education must prepare all students to live in the world of tomorrow. Students will be required during their lifetime to respond to more diversity than was dreamed of a few years ago. They have to respond to this diversity with both sensitivity and rationality. . . . International education must be also of direct service to local communities. It must serve the manifest needs of our immediate communities and taxpayers and there must be non-credit offerings related to such immediate concerns as world affairs, ethnicity, and exotic cultures and travel. Such offerings could include short courses on current international issues, seminars on the heritage of ethnic groups, cultural needs involving art, music and dance and truly educational travel opportunities for those who will inevitably travel.[11]

In a draft statement on overseas academic programs, the Office of International Programs, SUNY, Albany, notes that "the State University considers study in other countries an integral and valuable part of its academic offerings."[12] The paper specifically raises the question, why study abroad? Since this question is frequently asked, particularly in times of budgetary restrictions and taxpayers' concerns, the draft statement provides a number of answers:

1. Study in another country is the most dramatic and effective means of adding a very important international dimension to one's education and experience.
2. Overseas studies broadens perspectives in any field of study and provides important and unique contents in many.
3. It is one of the quickest and best ways of learning to use a foreign language.
4. It is an ideal means of understanding other cultures, people and their problems.
5. It gives perspectives on the United States and its relationships and problems in the interdependent world in which we live.
6. It enhances knowledge and appreciation of history, the arts and cultural differences.
7. It helps individual students to achieve maturity, self-reliance and broadens interest.
8. Many students returning from overseas study report that it has been the most valuable and exciting experience of their lives and it can often be done at little more cost than one would have as a resident student on his or her own campus.[13]

A third paper, issued by the International Studies and World Affairs Committee of SUNY, addressed itself specifically to the international commitment or the lack thereof in community colleges:

Since we live in a world increasingly interdependent, the international dimension is relevant to education at *all levels* in order to identify and provide means for comprehension and confrontation of the various problems facing humanity. The two-year college is commonly viewed as a local institution emphasizing technical and vocational programs. In fact, the curriculum offerings of the two-year institutions are becoming increasingly diversified to meet a broad variety of students' interests and goals. The burgeoning number of two-year college students must no longer be denied access to international perspectives.[14]

The Committee then proposes the following resolution:

Be it resolved that the university faculty senate recommend to the Chancellor that he (One) urge each president of a two-year college to make available to faculty and students, information about international education programs through catalogues, student handbooks, student organizations, newsletters as well as through the academic vice president, the director of international education and academic advisors and through any other means locally feasible. (Two), encourage administrators, faculty and students to use available resources to develop international dimensions of their college programs both academic and nonacademic. (Three), reaffirm the desirability of instructional sharing of faculty, staff and other resources. (Four), request the presidents of the two-year colleges to include summaries of international education developments in their annual report.[15]

The same paper, in its conclusion, proposes an amendment to the SUNY master plan on international education:

Recognizing the growing interdependence of the nations of the world and emphasizing the great educational and cultural value of international contact among students and faculty the university will continue to advance its substantial commitment to international education. A systematic university-wide evaluation will be made of the international components of academic programs and research and service activities at an appropriate time. Strong areas and other international education studies programs will be continued and the university will encourage expanding the relevant international content of academic programs. Special attention will be given to two-year colleges and to increasing regional and statewide inter-campus cooperation. Increased effort will be made to expand the size of the foreign student group through the university and corresponding effort will be made to assist increasing numbers of state university students to benefit from foreign study opportunities. Admission and financial support for foreign students will reflect two objectives of the university. One, to encourage the generosity of those countries which have provided subsidies for students from the university who have studied in their countries and, two, to recognize the contribution made by a diverse group of foreign students toward an enrichment of campus life. Each campus will be encouraged to make increased use of the relevant experience of faculty and students returning from study abroad and of the special knowledge of visiting foreign faculty and students.[16]

3.   The Rockland Model

In the previous chapter we considered the arguments for extending international educational programs to second-year and even first-year students. Now we must search out an innovative institution that has successfully experimented with an international program.

Rockland Community College (RCC) was selected as a model and, indeed, became known as the *Rockland Model,* because it was one of the first community colleges and perhaps the most successful in overseas academic programming. The college quickly assumed a leadership position, first among community colleges in New York State and then nationwide.

Rockland Community College, part of the State University of New York (SUNY) system, "is located in an attractive rural setting five miles east of Suffern, New York, and twenty-five miles north of New York City. The College is easily accessible from both the New York State Thruway and the Palisades Interstate Parkway."[1] Besides the main campus,[2] Rockland Community College leases or owns additional facilities and space for satellite units in Nyack, Spring Valley, and Haverstraw, New York.

As a comprehensive two-year college, RCC's degree programs are registered with the New York State Department of Education and approved by the State University of New York. The College is authorized to award the Associate in Arts and the Associate in Applied Science degrees as established by the Board of Regents of the University of the State of New York.[3] Rockland is accredited by the Middle States Association of Colleges and Secondary Schools. The College opened its doors to its first group of students in September 1959.

That start was the culmination of a five-year effort on the part of many educators, officials, and citizens throughout the area interested "in the possibility of some form of post-high school education for the youth and adults of the county."[4] A steering committee of about fifty members studied the community-college idea for about three years and assessed the need, interest, and support of Rockland County residents for establishment of a local college. The final report of the committee, presented to the Rockland County Board of Supervisors in March of 1959, concluded with the following statement: "A community college is needed and wanted in Rockland County and should be established so that the doors may be open to students in September 1959."[5]

A month later, in April, the Rockland County Board of Supervisors voted to establish a community college on the basis of this report, and in May of the same year the Board of Trustees of the State University granted approval. Rockland Community College is administered by "a Board of Trustees consisting of nine members, five appointed by the legislature of Rockland County and four appointed by the governor of the State of New York for terms of nine years."[6] According to community-college law,[7] RCC provides "two-year programs of post-high school nature combining general education with technical education . . . special courses and extension work [and] sufficient general education to enable qualified students who so desire to transfer after the completion of the program to institutions providing regular four-year courses."[8] The cost of operating the college "is shared 40% by the state, not more than one-third by the students in the form of tuition, and the balance by Rockland County and other counties of New York from which its students come. Capital costs are shared equally by the State and Rockland County."[9] It was the initiative of the State University of New York that provided the original stimulus for the development of the first academic programs overseas at Rockland Community College.

In 1967, RCC (like all other campuses in the SUNY system) was prompted to internationalize its curriculum, encourage the study of foreign languages, consider area studies, and begin to develop overseas academic programs for its students. The Central Administration of the State University of New York felt strongly that, as the largest university in the country, it had an obligation to experiment and forge new paths in higher education by introducing a sizable international dimension into the entire SUNY system.

This international program was intended not solely as a means of fulfilling the intellectual ambitions and broadening the academic perspectives of SUNY students. New York is a state with vast business connections reaching from New York City throughout the nation and the world, as well as a port of entry for a large number of immigrants from abroad. The SUNY administration felt it was in the state's business interest to define an international component in the State University as indispensable, without which the purposes of state higher education could not be well accomplished.

In its network of seventy-four higher educational institutions in 1967, the State University of New York included thirty-eight community colleges.[10] Out of a student population of 226,022 (defined as "total credit course students") in the entire SUNY system at that time, more than half, namely 115,500, were attending community colleges, with the majority of this group transferring to upper division colleges upon completion of their studies. SUNY Central clearly realized that it would be impossible to exclude the community colleges from the reach of the contemplated international activities.[11]

One college, far from being a mere accessory to the program, became one of its chief proponents and most successful implementers. Rockland Community College did not differ substantially in either history or organization from other community colleges in the state system. It was therefore considered roughly equivalent to other colleges when instructed by SUNY Central Administration to add an international dimension to its offerings. The intention of the state was to ensure that each of its institutions would develop an international component.

What the framers of the proposal did not take into account was that by the time of the inception of these programs the college had already established a reputation for innovation and experimentation under the leadership of a creative, dynamic, and dedicated president. Thus, the overseas academic programs at Rockland began to take shape in a setting somewhat different from that of other colleges in the system.

Two years earlier, in 1965, the State University of New York had established a Center for the purpose of drawing together all of SUNY's international efforts. This Center, located in Planting Fields, Long Island, and named International Studies and World Affairs (ISWA),[12] was to coordinate SUNY's international program. ISWA also served as clearinghouse, catalyst, and quality-control mechanism. Overseas academic programs were to originate on a SUNY campus with ISWA providing advice and expertise during the inauguration of these programs. No program was to be put into operation without final clearance from the Center. This procedure provided SUNY with the machinery to (1) avoid duplication of programs in particularly desirable locales abroad such as Paris or London; (2) check on these programs through quality-control mechanisms; and (3) provide Central Administration with a comprehensive picture of overseas academic activities within the total SUNY system. ISWA could fulfill these functions without threatening the authority and independence of individual campuses. A balance was struck between centralized and individual college control that enabled each college to develop its own program.

All the colleges, including RCC, were urged to establish an Office of International Education (OIE). This office was to work in cooperation with ISWA, and the Director of the Rockland OIE was to serve as liaison between the college and SUNY in all areas of international education.

At that time, most of the four-year SUNY colleges had already developed a variety of international activities, predominantly overseas academic programs, based largely on the Junior Year Abroad model. In addition, the four University Centers of SUNY[13] conducted graduate programs abroad. These already existing activities were to be coordinated through ISWA, and guidelines for the establishment of new programs and activities were to be developed and introduced. Since the university centers, four-year colleges, and technical and specialized colleges are centrally funded, it was not too difficult to establish liaison between these units making the free interchange of students among the various programs within the system possible.

SUNY hoped, thus, to make all of its overseas programs available to all SUNY students in all of the four-year units and university centers. In theory, the idea was perfect. In actuality, however, a number of problems emerged, such as recruitment, transfer, responsibility, and academic standards. These problems were not insurmountable, though, and did not seriously threaten the concept of student exchanges among four-year colleges and university centers.

For the community colleges in the SUNY system, however, the situation was radically different. Several important problems made the immediate introduction of overseas academic activities virtually impossible. The first and perhaps most substantial problem was a financial one. Because of a different funding structure, the State's community colleges could not operate overseas on the same basis as four-year colleges or SUNY centers. The absence of central funding created procedural difficulties in paying for instructional services abroad from local community-college budgets.

Second, there was a total absence of clear-cut guidelines for overseas academic activities on the community-college level. No procedure to provide for the maintenance of these programs had been established by either SUNY Central Administration or the community colleges themselves.

Third, faculty and community inertia, indifference, perhaps even resistance, had to be overcome, a most difficult task for many of the community colleges.

None of the community colleges had any experience with a comprehensive international program abroad prior to the period under discussion. There were a few faculty members in the system who had traveled abroad with groups of students and thereby developed some international interests. The individual activities usually were not part of the college curricula and often lacked serious academic content, structure, or continuity.

Rockland identified the problems, recognized the difficulties, and attempted to develop new administrative procedures to make overseas academic education possible for its students. In the process of establishing new guidelines, Rockland went through an intensive review and evaluation of the philosophy and goals of international education at the community-college level. The college was gradually able to develop orderly procedures, rules and regulations governing overseas academic programs, which established their place in the curriculum.

The RCC guidelines encompassed pilot projects; research into various geographical areas to assess their desirability for inclusion in the program; directives as to the size of student groups, financial viability, program duration, and administrative control; and, finally, the process of evaluation. Many of these rules and regulations were copied or adapted by other community colleges in the SUNY system.

Even more important than the procedural guidelines were the mechanics of financing these programs. As stated above, this problem did not exist for four-year colleges because of the method of funding these institutions. All tuition money from four-year colleges is pooled, and overseas international costs are paid out of the general college budget. It is this procedure that makes the transfer of students from one campus to another possible.

SUNY community colleges are not centrally funded; students pay their fees directly to the college. A student enrolled in a program overseas while remaining a student of record on his home campus had to pay the cost of instruction abroad in addition to his home-college tuition. This was not only a financial hardship to the student, but also actually in contravention of law. The student was asked to pay tuition twice, once to his home campus from which he was actually absent, and once to the foreign institution at which de facto instruction took place. Thus, unless procedures similar to those at four-year colleges could be worked out, no community college could successfully operate overseas academic programs.

Instructional costs for the programs overseas had to be made part of the regular operating budget of a community college so that tuition monies could be used to pay instructional fees abroad. Thus, Rockland was faced, along with other community colleges, with a huge financial and administrative hurdle.

Because Rockland made a special commitment to international programs, it attempted to resolve the administrative block through a series of insistent petitions to SUNY authorities. Almost one year of effort was necessary to obtain the ruling, which became the modus operandi for Rockland and all other community colleges in the SUNY system.

A memorandum from the vice-chancellor for two-year colleges finally resolved the problem. Dated August 12, 1970, it established the rule that if an overseas program was duly approved by Rockland, and reviewed and endorsed by the State University, instructional costs could be made part of the college's regular operating budget. Payments to meet the expenses were to be made in the same manner that bills were met for other authorized services. From that date on, all overseas activities conducted by and out of the Office of International Education at RCC could be treated *as if* these programs were conducted on campus. Overseas academic activities became part of the regular operating budget of the college. It was a significant breakthrough. From then on, Rockland and all SUNY community colleges were able to fund their international programs on the same basis that four-year colleges and university centers had long enjoyed.

Another difficulty RCC faced at the beginning was the faculty's lack of exposure to international education. Faculty members at community colleges are often indifferent to internationalization of subject matter and the international involvement of the community college itself. Sponsors of these programs had to arouse interest and support among individual faculty members. The faculty had to be convinced that these programs were in the best interest of the departments and the college. With new students gained and new programs generated over time, international programs did prove to be a valuable addition to the academic departments. It was easier to appeal to the students. By working directly with the RCC Student Senate, sponsors gained the cooperation and interest of the students.

Close cooperation with the Evening and Extension Division of the college brought forth further support, first from community leaders and later the community at large. Thus, important local forces reinforced the desired impact on the college faculty. It was recognized from the start that without cooperation, support, and active involvement of the faculty, such programs could not be successfully mounted.

Internal barriers to the successful establishment of viable overseas programs were recognized and, over time, removed at Rockland. The same problems had to be dealt with at other community colleges and were resolved, with some differences there as well. Once the philosophical, administrative and financial hurdles at Rockland were substantially overcome, overseas academic programs on the community-college level could be put into operation. An international dimension was added that would make it possible for RCC to fulfill its function of educating the community internationally in the last quarter of the century. The demands of an increasingly interdependent world were thus recognized in the region served by the college.

The first and major step was to build programs abroad. An attempt was made to give the college immediate visibility through its presence abroad. In fairly rapid succession, overseas international programs in a variety of academic subjects were created. Several of these were short-term programs (less than one semester), easier to mount and finance in a limited period of time. Semester-long programs were developed shortly thereafter, until the full complement of students in the international program was reached.

Because of the limited foreign-language abilities of community-college students, it was natural to look toward England as the first country where programs abroad could be developed. Accordingly, that is where the first short-term as well as semester-long programs at RCC were established. In time the circle widened. The program became perhaps too Eurocentric; but the language factor and the high cost of transportation to places beyond Europe make such a concentration understandable. As noted above, it is also natural that descendants of Europeans would favor study programs in European countries over those in other regions.

The early short-term programs provided faculty members as well as students with their first overseas experience and developed a skeleton staff for later long-term ventures. While the academic content of these programs was closely circumscribed by New York State Education Department curriculum guidelines, the actual format of each experience had to be developed at the college through close cooperation between the academic departments involved and the Director of International Education (DIE). The present range of programs is a product of cumulative growth of these overseas opportunities.

For the future it is hoped that the Office of International Education at RCC can respond to demand as the need arises, while maintaining or enlarging the variety and volume of existing programs. A representative short-term program is presented below as an illustration of the international component at RCC.

One of the first and perhaps most successful short-term programs at Rockland was a Criminal Justice Seminar, developed in close cooperation with the chairman of the Criminal Justice Department at RCC. When this two-week intersession program was started, scheduled to take place between the fall and spring semester of each year, no one at the college knew for certain if such a seminar was academically viable enough for college credits to be awarded. It was therefore decided to conduct the *first* seminar in January 1971 as a workshop only (no academic credits), with the chairman of the Criminal Justice Department participating in the program for the purpose of evaluating its academic content and benefit to the students. He would thus be able to make a sound judgment regarding the credits to be attached to that seminar in the future.

Upon his return, he was convinced that an academically revised and improved seminar should, indeed, be offered for academic credit during the intersession a year later.

This intersession Criminal Justice Seminar, over a period of ten years, turned out to be the most successful program, in terms of numbers of students, offered in this time period by RCC overseas. The reasons for the success of that particular seminar are several; the most important ones are listed in the following paragraphs.

First, the chairman of the department was actively and deeply involved in the program and its success from the beginning. He was constantly establishing new contacts in London while keeping close ties with the various institutions and agencies he was utilizing for the program.

Second, when the Criminal Justice Seminar grew substantially in numbers of students, RCC was notified by the London Home Office that the demands of the program had started to seriously hamper orderly police procedures in London. Thus, a directive from the Home Office restricted visiting Criminal Justice programs to active police officers formally sponsored by their professional organizations in the United States. Largely through the efforts of the British police union, and with the assistance of the British embassy in Washington and the American embassy in London, formal sponsorship for the RCC program was achieved so that the number of participating students in the seminar could be increased even further. Thus, adversity was turned into support.

Third, the reception of the program in London now is such that RCC is the only college allowed to offer participating police officers actual attachment services, a procedure whereby American police officers are "attached" to their counterparts working out of police precincts in London and its environs. The "partners" cooperate closely, usually for a number of days. These attachments are worked out by Home Office police officials prior to the arrival of the group, testifying to the support this program receives from the various police agencies and academies in London.

Fourth, the close cooperation between British police-training schools and Rockland has been strengthened over the years by the fact that the Criminal Justice Department at the college has played host to a variety of police groups as well as individual police officers and their families from Britain. This interchange of social and professional contacts has greatly facilitated the task of making the RCC Criminal Justice program in London perhaps the best program of its kind.

We add to the description of the Criminal Justice program in England a brief comment about a related program, also in London, for secretarial students. Because of changed labor conditions in England, which resulted in countermanding of work permits for foreign secretaries, this program unfortunately no longer exists. However, it was a breakthrough at the time, since it was the first and only work-study program abroad of any community college in the United States. In it, students were required to work for six weeks, under supervision, in a variety of offices in London, while attending classes conducted by an RCC faculty member twice a week in the evening. The students were paid current London wages for office temporaries. Although the pay was not sufficient to meet all their expenses, it did help to offset the cost substantially. Students paid for their transportation to and from England and had to maintain themselves in London. At the end of the six-week study period, students could, if they wished, remain on the job for three more weeks, though no further classes were held, or they could remain in London without working. As a third choice, students could travel on their own in Europe. The program ended after a nine-week period. Academic credits were awarded on the basis of the work experience gained and the academic classes attended during the first six weeks. It is regrettable that this thriving program had to terminate simply because of changed economic conditions in the host country, a situation beyond the control of Rockland Community College.

The prevailing style at the college, with very few exceptions, was to establish short-term programs first. Then, after these were found to operate successfully, the experience and contacts were utilized to develop long-term offerings. The reasons are self-evident. This sequence follows the established pattern of successful overseas academic programming generally. Because of the complexities of financing, cost to the student, academic credits, and methods of supervision and evaluation, it was advantageous to utilize established contacts and known facilities to decrease the problems involved in building semester- or even year-long programs. For these offerings special attention had to be paid along several lines of policy.

First, students must be more carefully selected. If a student is misplaced in an overseas short-term assignment, the loss of learning experience can be made up in academic credits after his return to the home campus. If, on the other hand, a similar misplacement of a student occurs in a long-term program, the result would be the waste of an entire academic semester and losses in academic credits and time.

Second, disruptive or misplaced students cause comparatively little harm to short-term ventures abroad. But in a long-term situation, one or two individuals with psychological or personal problems can easily complicate the smooth operation, well-being, and functioning of the entire group placed overseas.

Fourth, while the short-term programs involve and, in-

deed, intrigue faculty members because they provide
them with the opportunity to be directly involved in
travel, teaching, and supervision, it would be against the
very spirit and philosophy of overseas academic programs
to have home-campus courses taught by home-campus
faculty members abroad. Since foreign faculty must replace them, the interest of the home-campus faculty in
semester programs overseas is less pronounced. In fact,
they may view these programs as competitive, perhaps
even a threat to their own courses and, therefore, may be
reluctant to cooperate and support them. For these and
other reasons,[14] the construction of long-term programs
requires extra care and better planning.

An example of a long-term program developed at RCC
is presented here to demonstrate how these difficulties can
be resolved. In 1972, Rockland sent its first contingent of
eighteen students with one instructor to Jerusalem to study
at the now defunct American College in Jerusalem. The
American College was a four-year liberal-arts college
chartered in the United States. It offered a standard four-
year liberal-arts curriculum with a heavy infusion of
courses on Israeli culture and history and Jewish religion.

For the next two years, the number of Rockland students in Israel remained fairly stable, fluctuating between
seventeen and thirty per semester. The RCC faculty member remained as program director in Israel for those two
years. When it became clear, during the second year of
operation, that the American College in Jerusalem was
experiencing financial difficulties, the RCC faculty member in residence started to establish contacts with other
educational institutions in Israel. Also, by that time a new
"philosophy" had started to take shape at RCC regarding
the Israel program. It had become evident that the program in operation could not absorb the rather wide spec-

trum of students who applied for study in Israel. For some of the students, the program offerings were not broad enough, while to others they did not sufficiently emphasize Jewish studies. Thus, RCC started to look for ways that would enable the college to match students with the kinds of programs and institutions in Israel that would meet their requirements as well as their intellectual and academic capabilities. Rockland wanted to develop an "academic linkage service" in Israel.

When the RCC faculty member returned to the home campus, he brought with him commitments from twelve educational institutions in Israel that were willing to accept Rockland students in a wide variety of subjects. During the following academic year RCC maintained its program in Israel with fewer students and a local person supervising it.

The former Rockland program director now started to offer this academic linkage service to agencies and groups in the New York area with the result that, one year later, RCC sent 126 full-time students to Israel to study at sixteen different educational institutions. The number of participating institutions in Israel had been increased from twelve to sixteen during that same academic year.

The key for the rapid increase in the number of participating students in the various programs offered in Israel was the availability of a large variety of educational institutions and programs that could meet the individual needs of different types of students.

One significant result of Rockland's program in Israel has been the creation of "Mat'eh Yehudah," a service-learning[15] college without walls sponsored by Rockland Community College. Mat'eh Yehudah is a community of 22,000 in the Jerusalem Corridor in Israel, composed largely of Jews of Oriental origin. The Regional Council of Mat'eh Yehudah created a "Midrashah," a regional college and then invited RCC to create an American-type college without walls in collaboration with the entire region of Mat'eh Yehudah. The program at the college is designed and administered by RCC with the Regional Council providing opportunities for student work, placement, and housing.

RCC and the "Midrashah" share an educational center at Ein Karem. The college is designed to bring students from the United States and all over the world to "serve and learn" in Israel. The project was developed as an alternative for students who wish to combine classroom instruction with the opportunity to work, thereby enabling the students to learn and practice specific career skills while contributing to the region in which they live.

The work may be devoted wholly to specific fieldwork related to the student's area of study, as described in his individualized learning contract, or it may consist of teaching English to the adults and children of the region or a combination of the two. It should be noted that the learning contract[16] at Mat'eh Yehudah is a very rigorous academic undertaking requiring imagination, self-discipline, planning, maturity, and emotional stability.

While working and living with families or in student accommodations, students receive a stipend to cover incidental living expenses. The program is designed to unite education and work so that the student is simultaneously learning and doing. Mat'eh Yehudah is the only college of its kind developed in Israel by an American community college.

In surveying the short-term and semester-long programs overseas which have burgeoned at RCC since 1971, it can be seen that constant growth has been their most significant characteristic. There is uncertainty now as to whether continued growth is desirable or is needed to maintain the momentum the program has enjoyed. Perhaps these programs should be stabilized at an optimum size and simply take their place in the regular pattern of academic life on the RCC campus.

However this question may be resolved, it is clear that the program's most notable achievement to date has been its ability to provide a variety of offerings in different countries and cultures to a great number of students with differing backgrounds, aspirations, and levels of academic preparation. Whenever the conditions of the receiving country or program could not be matched with students' needs, there was sufficient flexibility to create new opportunities or modify existing ones. RCC has thus created a vital organization capable of expansion or adjustment to external conditions. Rockland's dynamic, innovative approach has enabled it to overcome hurdles not faced by four-year institutions in the creation of an international education program within the framework of the community college.

The successful formula for the establishment and development of international academic programs on the community-college level seems to depend on the following three conditions:

1. The support and commitment of the chief administrative officer.
2. The support of the faculty.
3. The presence of a catalyst in the person of the local director of international education, who can function largely because of administrative support and faculty cooperation.

These three ingredients have been instrumental in ensuring the success of the overseas venture at Rockland Community College. It is recalled that the original stimulus for the introduction of overseas academic programs at RCC came not from within but from without. This outside stimulus fell on fertile ground at Rockland because the three conditions listed above were present. The very same stimulus did not initiate activities at many other community colleges because these conditions were either wholly or partially absent.

Philosophically, these programs were and are aimed at providing the students with experiences consistent with community-college aims and policy—the delicate weaving together of academic study, vocational and professional activities, and work experience. To maintain this balance between the conflicting forces of regionalism and internationalism requires vision, determination, leadership, and commitment to the principles of globalism in today's world. One thing seems certain: The experience of Rockland Community College with a variety of short-term and long-term overseas programs suggests that community colleges are, contrary to their critics' beliefs, admirably suited to the origination and maintenance of successful overseas ventures. The tradition of a Junior Year Abroad is thereby put to rest as the sole means through which college students may experience foreign academic study. The culture of the people of the world is a common heritage from which community-college students, many of whose ambitions do not include the gaining of a college degree, may no longer be excluded.

4. Interinstitutional, State, and National Cooperation

It has been shown that successful overseas academic programs are a viable possibility for sophomores and even freshmen in a community college. An immediate and important question has to be asked: Can the operation just described be successfully exported or is it necessarily confined to a single community college, simply because of the congruence of a set of favorable conditions particular to one specific college? It is common knowledge that the best educational systems do not always survive nor can they always be successfully transplanted.[1] The answer to this question, which is expanded upon in the rest of this book, is decidedly in the affirmative.

Rockland Community College's success in establishing a dynamic academic program overseas for its students soon became well known. This reputation spread in ever-widening circles, first to the surrounding counties, then beyond the immediate area and into the state at large and, ultimately, beyond the state borders. It was like dropping a stone into a lake, with ever-widening ripples reaching a larger and larger area.

Rockland's influence on other colleges followed a pattern: First, a cooperative effort between RCC and other community colleges in the immediate region took place. Second, in a concentric pattern, cooperation began to extend to other community colleges in other areas. Third, four-year colleges in the state system worked constructively with RCC. Fourth, the radiation process began to extend beyond the state of New York into surrounding states and even onto the national scene.

At the same time, Rockland was increasingly invited to participate in State University Councils on International Education, and more and more attention was paid to the contributions it could make to these meetings. This chapter narrates the cooperative effort between Rockland Community College and other educational institutions, both inside and outside the state of New York.

COOPERATION WITH OTHER COMMUNITY COLLEGES WITHIN THE SUNY SYSTEM

From the beginning of its involvement in international programs, the College strongly believed in interinstitutional cooperation on all levels and has managed to translate that conviction into reality in various ways. The first step was to involve a number of community colleges, also affiliates of the State University of New York, located near RCC. At once a number of questions had to be answered. Did the administrative guidelines developed at one college transfer smoothly to other colleges? Could the financial procedures work equally well in other institutions? Would the commitment of the chief administrative officer be strong enough? Could the cooperation of the faculty be elicited to conduct these programs? Was it possible to identify a faculty member or administrator who could successfully direct all international efforts? Experience and time have provided rather definite answers. The first two questions, administrative and financial, can be answered with an unqualified yes, while the remaining three need further elaboration.

The administrative guidelines transferred rather smoothly from one community college to another for three simple reasons:

1. The community college administrations within the State system are similarly structured.
2. The guidelines carried the sanction of SUNY Central Administration.
3. They were the only guidelines available.

The financial procedures developed for the funding of instructional costs overseas also could be applied by other community colleges. But first it was necessary to thoroughly familiarize the chief financial officer of each institution with the mechanics of the operation. Again, existing SUNY Central Administration approval facilitated the transfer.

It is one thing to transfer guidelines and procedures from one institution to another, but it is a vastly different matter to pass on intangibles such as commitment of leaders, enthusiasm and conviction of the faculty, and administrative know-how, all of which are important in the selection of staff. Again, three rules emerged.

1. Since the support of the chief administrative officer of an institution is a necessary prerequisite in a venture such as overseas academic programming, Rock-

land awaited invitations for cooperation from other institutions. Thus, the positive predisposition of the president of the inviting college could be assumed.

2. The selection of a suitable Director of International Education at a community college is of crucial importance. If at all possible, he or she should come from the ranks of the faculty, since other faculty members are more likely to wholeheartedly support a program headed by one of their fellows. Experience in several SUNY four-year colleges has clearly demonstrated that "outsiders" have a very difficult time overcoming the skepticism of faculty. They must devote an extraordinary amount of time convincing the teaching staff that they can handle questions of academic quality, credits, transfer, grades, and contact hours. In addition, the director should have organizational talent and a desire to work in administration—at first on a part-time basis—since most community colleges simply do not need the services of a full-time DIE when starting out. Finally, the person has to be totally committed to international education, since it is this commitment that will carry him or her through initial difficulties and help solve constantly emerging problems.

3. To elicit support and cooperation from the majority of faculty members inevitably turned out to be the most difficult problem. It is the faculty who pass on the enthusiasm for overseas programs to students. Therefore, faculty must be persuaded and thoroughly educated about the program. Initial conferences with faculty members can spark momentary interest; that interest, however, must be sustained. It is the responsibility of the local DIE to work with the faculty and elicit their cooperation. The

help and support of the president of the college in this effort is of course invaluable. In some community colleges this task turned out to be impossible.

One example will support the rules stated above. Community College X, located in a neighboring county, invited the Rockland DIE to spend a day on campus to discuss problems of adding an international component to the existing curriculum. During the visit, discussions and conferences were arranged with administrative officials, including the president of the college, the director of finance, and several deans, chairmen, and faculty members. At the conclusion of these meetings, the premise of introducing international education dimensions at Community College X had been generally accepted.

The next step was a decision to have a contingent of faculty members visit Rockland to discuss specifically the operation of overseas academic programs. RCC faculty members participating in the ensuing daylong discussions had all conducted programs abroad. Following that second meeting, held on the RCC campus, College X decided to participate actively with RCC in the intersession seminars to be offered in London less than three months later.

Faculty were to participate according to certain guidelines that would smooth cooperative efforts. The guidelines stipulated that the faculty member conducting the seminar in London should come from the college contributing the largest number of students to the program. Should several colleges each fill a section of at least fifteen students, each campus would provide its own faculty member to supervise its own section of the program. The actual teaching abroad is done mostly by British instructors and experts in the field.

During the upcoming intersession, twenty-eight students and two faculty members from Community College X participated in the London program. Close cooperation between the two colleges continued, and the following year College X conducted two new seminars of its own in London. These additional programs were open to RCC students, just as the Rockland seminars offered in London were open to students from College X. Thus, Rockland helped to introduce another community college to international education.

After this successful introduction, the person responsible for the initial cooperation effort at College X was designated as the local DIE. The college granted the new director, a tenured faculty member, a reduction in his teaching course load. At the end of the academic year, the chairman of the board at College X noted in his commencement address that the college had added international programs as a new dimension to the curriculum. The cooperative link between the two community colleges was thus permanently established.

Similar attempts with other SUNY community colleges have taken place, although not all of these colleges have pursued the initial contact with the same commitment, dedication, and success shown by College X. Perhaps the main attraction of Rockland to other community colleges in the SUNY system was the fact that, through cooperation, they could avoid the considerable expense involved in developing and mounting programs overseas on their own. In addition, these colleges could learn from Rockland's experience and avoid mistakes.

Most importantly, overseas academic programs are financially viable only if at least fifteen students enroll. Not many small colleges can muster this number in the beginning. Some community colleges therefore placed a few of their students in the Rockland programs, thus limiting their initial investment.

Not all of the community colleges that sought assistance from Rockland succeeded in their efforts as did Community College X, described above. Failures can be ascribed to one or more of the following three reasons:

1. The commitment and support of the administration, notably the president, was lacking or not strong enough to sustain an ongoing enterprise.
2. The DIE did not have enough leverage and support to see the effort through or was unable to elicit the necessary faculty cooperation on a permanent basis.
3. Institutional rivalry stood in the way; some institutions attempted to pursue their own independent programs despite the financial disadvantages. Regrettably, most such independent efforts by other community colleges failed.

COOPERATION WITH STATE COLLEGES

The first phase of successful sharing involved Rockland with other community colleges, first in the immediate region and later in the state at large. Cooperation among two-year institutions in building and conducting overseas academic programs thus was shown to be possible. The second phase involved cooperation between RCC and the four-year colleges and university centers within SUNY. The difficulties in such cooperation arose in part from the operational differences in overseas academic programming among the various units.

The internal structure, history, and method of financing of upper-division SUNY units differ greatly from those of two-year institutions. One crucial difference involved the position of the DIE.

From the time the State University started to become interested in international education, almost all efforts were concentrated on the four-year colleges and university centers. Community-college Directors of International Education were always invited to the SUNY semester meetings, but most discussions concerned only the upper-division colleges. In addition, SUNY had allocated line positions for DIEs on all campuses except the community colleges. These lines were not filled in all instances by full-time personnel and, in a few isolated cases, were not occupied at all, but the creation of these positions made it possible to develop a cadre of DIEs that insured continuity and cooperation among the membership.

Unfortunately, this was not the case at community colleges. No positions were created by SUNY, and the establishment of an Office of International Education on each campus and the designation of a Director for that office was left to the president of each community college.

As a result, very few two-year colleges had even a part-time Director of International Education, and those few experienced considerable turnover. Thus, the community college DIE group of participants at general SUNY meetings was not only very small but also unstable. They had little leverage to make themselves and their problems heard and understood or move in concert toward the introduction of international components on all community-college campuses.

The situation was different at Rockland. There, the first Director initially occupied the position in addition to a full teaching load, but after several years, a permanent full-time DIE position was established. This enabled RCC to build up the program described in the preceding chapter and to initiate interinstitutional cooperation within SUNY. Rockland Community College, from the beginning, sought cooperation with four-year institutions. This cooperation was facilitated by the regular participation of the Rockland DIE in the SUNY-wide meetings and conferences on overseas programs.

As the only permanent spokesman for community colleges in these meetings, the Rockland DIE was elected to the SUNY Executive Committee on International Education.[2] He was then in an even better position to work with DIEs from the university centers and four-year colleges in the system.

Many of these colleges in SUNY already had active and successful overseas academic programs when Rockland entered the scene. These programs were mostly on the junior-year level, although some included sophomores. As a newcomer, RCC could profit from the experiences of the upper-division colleges, but it had to adapt this information to the special demands of the community college. Their program had to be directed to a younger clientele.

Initial imitation was soon replaced by cooperation. Rockland established an excellent working relationship with four-year colleges; an example of one successful and mutually beneficial relationship is related below.

Empire State College, SUNY's college without walls, operates out of a number of Learning Centers largely on the contract method. A student, together with his academic mentor, develops and signs a learning contract, and upon its fulfillment he receives academic credits and ultimately a college degree. After Rockland had been operating a successful liberal-arts semester program in England for several years, Empire State College decided to transplant its mentor system to London. When Empire State

opened a Learning Center in London, the two institutions
started to cooperate successfully. In the beginning, the
Empire State mentor supervised RCC's students in London when RCC did not have a faculty member stationed
there.

During the following two years, after Rockland started
again to maintain a faculty representative in London,
faculty members from the two colleges worked together
closely, sharing resources, programs, and study opportunities. Soon a joint London Learning Center was established. This shared facility in London provided a number
of important benefits:

1. Costs were effectively cut by sharing facilities abroad.
2. A four-year state operated (centrally funded)
   SUNY unit successfully cooperated with a locally
   funded SUNY community college.
3. The common facilities improved the quality of academic offerings overall.
4. New and innovative types of programs emerged.

As a result, RCC started to use the contract and mentor
system abroad, adapting it to serve community-college
students. With the vast learning resources available in
London, contract studies could now be offered to both
lower- and upper-division students. Following the London
example, Empire State College and Rockland Community
College cooperated just as successfully for several years
in Israel.

Rockland's work with other community colleges and
four-year units within the SUNY system culminated in
the suggestion of a drastic change in policy in Albany.
RCC proposed that all freshmen and sophomores in the
system would participate in overseas academic programs
through community colleges only. Lower-division (first-

and second-year) students enrolled in four-year colleges and university centers who wanted to study abroad would receive a one-semester leave of absence from their home campuses. The credits earned in the community-college program overseas were to be transferred to their respective upper-division colleges. The advantage to the four-year colleges was that some of their funds would be freed and could be used for their junior and senior students overseas.

For several reasons—faculty resistance, lack of coordination, college autonomy, and budgetary questions—the policy change was never implemented. However, the serious consideration of the proposal testifies to the quality of work abroad performed by the SUNY community colleges.

MULTISTATE COOPERATION—
THE TRI-STATE CONSORTIUM

The success of Rockland's international programs, specifically its progress in eliciting support from the state and cooperation from other SUNY units, suggested to planners at RCC the possibility of exporting these activities beyond the borders of New York State.

Rockland's efforts in this field had already been noticed and appreciated in religious quarters. A group of Protestant churches, which form the Ecumenical Council of New York, was concerned about the decrease in persons entering the ministry and the empty church facilities in this country and in Europe. It was thought that college students would put the church properties to good use, at the same time promoting desirable international understanding.

These laudable intentions coincided with a desire for

expansion at RCC. There, a search was underway for new sources of funding. Eventually, it was hoped, Rockland would qualify for federal support in its quest for international programs on the community-college level. However, as long as these programs were provided within New York State only, applications for federal funding were routinely referred back to the New York State Education Department.

Such were the circumstances surrounding the birth of the Tri-State Consortium. In 1972, RCC received a financial grant from the Ecumenical Council to be used "toward the establishment of interstate cooperation in the field of international education on the community college level."[3]

During exploratory discussions and planning sessions, RCC chose one community college each in New Jersey and Pennsylvania. Both were to serve as a "hub" for efforts to internationalize community colleges in the two states. As was the case in New York, it was hoped that after a start-up period the two community colleges would be able to draw similar institutions in their states into the circle. They were to occupy the same position Rockland occupied among community colleges within SUNY in particular and New York State in general.

A meeting of the presidents of the three colleges at Newark airport on July 31, 1972, laid the groundwork for the project. At that meeting it was decided that each president would nominate one person on his staff, responsible directly to the chief administrative officer of the college, to serve as liaison and coordinator of the newly formed Tri-State Consortium on International Education. Direct access to the decision-making officer at each college was, in retrospect, perhaps the single most important decision responsible for the success of the Tri-State Consortium.

The colleges in New Jersey and Pennsylvania were selected for specific reasons. The president of the college in Pennsylvania had established a reputation for himself and his college for innovativeness and administrative excellence. He was the author of several books on community-college administration and was nationally recognized as an expert in this field. The president of the New Jersey college had a longstanding commitment to innovation and cooperation similar to the philosophy at Rockland.

The assistants to the presidents at these two colleges were to act as liaison persons to the Tri-State Consortium, while at RCC the Director of International Education was to take on this additional responsibility. The fact that the three liaison persons had direct access to the presidents of the three member colleges provided the Consortium from the beginning with needed flexibility and the opportunity for quick action.

During the next January intersession period, the Consortium representatives from New Jersey and Pennsylvania accompanied a large group of Rockland students and faculty members to London to observe first-hand the RCC programs there. "Participant observation," it was thought, would constitute the best possible means to demonstrate to the two cooperating colleges the value, diversity, academic richness, and success of these international education activities for their own students and colleges.

The two Consortium members, thus exposed to actual academic activities overseas, returned to their campuses and started intensive efforts to develop similar programs. As a result, during the intersession period one year later, both colleges participated with RCC in a variety of seminars in Europe. Each member college in the Consortium now provided sizable numbers of students and several faculty members for these programs overseas.

This institutional cooperative effort across state lines worked very well, indeed. The variety of available overseas academic programs, the number of geographic locations for these ventures, and the student population enrolled in the programs increased rapidly. This dramatic upswing, especially in the number of students participating, could be attributed largely to the free-entry-permit system developed by the Consortium. According to this system, any program overseas conducted by any one of the three campuses was automatically open to all students enrolled in each of the three Consortium colleges. In order to achieve this interinstitutional enrollment, tuition structures and payment schedules in the three states had to be standardized. At the time, such cross-institutional funding constituted a real innovation and breakthrough.

The difficulties in channeling students from community colleges into overseas programs conducted by four-year colleges (or vice versa) within the SUNY system were described above. The ensuing problems of payment for instructional costs were complicated because of the differing funding methods in the two types of institutions—a central budget for four-year colleges and university centers and individual budgets for community colleges.

The difficulty was even greater in transferring instructional costs across state lines so that students from several states could participate in this ambitious interinstitutional program. The problem was solved astonishingly well and with relative speed through the so-called charge-back system, which operated as follows.

Each member college in the Tri-State Consortium on International Education charged its students their usual tuition and paid to the college conducting the program overseas the regular fees for instructional services. Frequently, no funds had to be exchanged, since the number of students from one campus enrolled in a program conducted by another college was often roughly equal to the number of students from the latter campus participating in a program conducted by the former. Instructional costs paid by one college were offset by instructional costs received from the other college for the latter's students.

The difficulties in organizing and maintaining the Tri-State Consortium were manageable, while the benefits to the students and the three colleges have been significant. In time, each of the three colleges started to draw other community colleges or students in these states into the Consortium. It was soon necessary* for the organization to expand its overseas program to accommodate the greater number of students who wished to enroll. Membership in the Consortium grew substantially in a relatively short time. From the original three members, the Consortium expanded to a total of ten community colleges in the three states. Of these, six were located in New York, three in New Jersey, and one in Pennsylvania. The concept of interinstitutional cooperation in overseas academic programming on the community-college level across state lines had been made to work.

NATIONAL COOPERATION

Within three years of its inception, the Tri-State Consortium on International Education became actively involved in the formation of another consortium, proposed by the Board of Directors of the American Association of Community and Junior Colleges (AACJC). This national

organization proceeded in 1975 to work toward "the establishment of a consortium of community and junior
colleges with special concerns in international and intercultural dimensions of education."[4] The AACJC advo-
cated that a consortium effort "would focus attention on
strengthening relevant college programs and services [in
the field of international education] and would help member institutions to share professional experiences with
nations requesting assistance as they develop their own
variations of middle-level tertiary institutions similar to
U.S. community and junior technical colleges."[5]

The AACJC proposed that community colleges with a
commitment in this field needed to pool their resources in
order to increase their potential for service through membership in a consortium arrangement. This national consortium proposed to render the following services, some
of which mirrored the original offerings of the Tri-State
Consortium on International Education:

1. Provide a clearinghouse of information on: interna-
   tional/intercultural programs and activities in junior
   and community colleges and other institutions; con-
   sultant opportunities abroad for junior and community college personnel; study-abroad programs for
   students and community members; requests for proposals from international agencies, other nations,
   federal agencies, and other offices.
2. Serve as spokesmen and advocates for the field representing its interests to World Bank, Agency for
   International Development, the U.S. Department of
   State, Inter-American Development Bank, founda-
   tions, foreign governments and embassy officials,
   higher education associations and international
   groups such as the Institute for International Edu-

cation, the National Association for Foreign Student Affairs, etc.

3. Assist colleges in developing international/intercultural dimensions of their curriculums and educational services in the U.S. and in other countries through research, conferences, liaison with other institutions and agencies.

4. Sponsor and coordinate efforts to help member colleges obtain study-abroad programs at lowest possible costs. (The Tri-State Consortium of Community Colleges, in Pennsylvania, New York, and New Jersey is willing to offer its services to other colleges to provide study-abroad opportunities in general as well as occupational-technical education in 15 countries with no administrative costs or charges.)

5. Maintain a file of individuals in the consortium colleges who are interested in professional consulting opportunities in other countries. Files would include language skills, professional experiences, and regional preferences, among others.

6. Serve as a channel to the many nations requesting advice and assistance in establishing junior or community college-type programs. A number of nations have recently requested information about services that might be purchased from the many AACJC-related colleges; and several countries hope to underwrite the costs of enrolling their own students in such colleges.

7. Sponsor conferences, both national and international, to focus on improving education-for-development programs.

8. Sponsor activities to help member colleges build sensitivity to and awareness of the growing interdependence of nations and the need for more effective education for world understanding among students and members of the communities at large.[6]

Note that the Tri-State Consortium of Community Colleges in New York, New Jersey, and Pennsylvania is specifically mentioned in the AACJC proposal (paragraph 4).

The newly created AACJC International/Intercultural Consortium (I/IC) published a number of position papers, one of which explained why community colleges were experiencing time lag in international education compared to four-year colleges and universities.[7]

Even though community colleges have grown in numbers from 678 in 1960 to over 1,200 in 1975,[8] the paper states that

> current guidelines under which USOE's [U.S. Office of Education] adoption of international education as well as the U.S. Department of State's Bureau of Education and Cultural Affairs, provided assistance for international programs of higher institutions were formulated during the critical years of the cold war period and for the benefit of institutions with potential in providing direct foreign policy resources for the cold war effort. Thus the broad public thrust of community and junior colleges, a non-target of these guidelines, together with their institutional units, preempted their partaking of the international education incentives provided by federal agencies.[9]

In spite of this handicap, community colleges in the United States have begun to develop international education programs in recent years and have tried to internationalize their curricula and develop cooperative educational programs. A survey of international and intercultural programs in two-year colleges conducted by the World Studies Data Bank of New York in cooperation with AACJC's Office of International Programs revealed the existence of 140 programs in approximately 200 colleges. During 1972–1975, "the numbers of types of . . . programs and colleges which incorporated a type of international/intercultural dimension have increased dramatically,"[10] an increase to which the Tri-State Consortium on International Education substantially contributed.

The rising interest in international education among community colleges can be traced partly to a new emphasis which "world dependencies are receiving and which in turn are calling for innovative ways of dealing with them."[11] The same position paper continues to list five community colleges across the country that form part of a larger core of community-based institutions that are committed to strengthening their international dimensions. Rockland Community College (one of the five colleges listed) "appears now as the leading college in offering study programs abroad, . . . [and] the genius of its internationalistic staff is increasingly sought by other colleges."[12]

It is evident from the foregoing narrative that RCC and the Tri-State Consortium were involved to a great degree in the creation of the AACJC International/Intercultural Consortium.

In an issue of the *Community and Junior College Journal,* the elected president of the AACJC paid tribute to the newly established Consortium when he noted, "it now comprises some 56 community colleges who have recognized that two-year institutions can gain much from community-based education from other nations—and hopes that we can offer something to other countries in the way of ideas, information and assistance."[13]

A number of college leaders appointed by the AACJC formed an advisory committee to set priorities for the national consortium, which included the following:

1. Provision of technical assistance to other countries interested in developing educational programs similar to those offered by community colleges.
2. Establishment of study/work/service programs abroad.
3. Inclusion of more institutions into existing international programs at consortium colleges.
4. Creation of an intercultural exchange program within the United States.

Thus, the AACJC "has established a base upon which the consortium can launch its program . . . [and] while the Association has many high program priorities, . . . we believe that a fair share of time and attention should be given to the international dimension. The AACJC International/Intercultural Consortium provides an excellent vehicle for realizing that goal—without neglect to the domestic scene."[14] It is gratifying to note that even in times of budget cuts and financial restrictions, the national leadership in the community-college field does include international education among its priorities.

Rockland Community College continued to play a national role in the international field. During the 56th Annual Conference of the AACJC in Washington, D.C., the International/Intercultural Consortium devoted two days to a series of meetings, workshops, panels, and discussions on international education.

The meetings were seen as answering the needs of a "growing group of community and junior colleges . . . coming together for the purpose of developing viable community college responses to pressing global issues that increasingly confront our community-based constituencies. To address these goals, the key approach that AACJC promotes is that of institutional linkages to facilitate access to the international expertise of member colleges by those that are experiencing an emerging interest in the experience of their counterparts."[15] The international staff of Rockland participated in many of these groups. For example, a panel discussion on "study/work abroad—new schemes for program sharing" was chaired by the director of RCC's Office of International Education. Panel members, including a second RCC participant and two members of the Tri-State Consortium, were:

1. the director of Cooperative Education, New Hampshire Community College;
2. the Vice-President for Academic Affairs, Broward Community College, Florida;
3. the Director of International Work Experience, West Valley Community College, California;
4. the Assistant to the President, Mercer Community College, New Jersey;
5. the Vice-President for Educational Services, Harrisburg Community College, Pennsylvania; and
6. the Coordinator, SUNY/Israel Project, Rockland Community College, New York.

This two-day workshop established the growing commitment of AACJC to international education and reinforced the linkage between the Tri-State Consortium on International Education and the national consortium established by the AACJC.

The impact of the consortium form of organization on international education in community colleges can be summarized in the following two ways: First, the potential for cooperation in international work can be demonstrated by the widening circles of the Rockland experience. Beginning on one college campus, the program soon reached out to other community colleges in the same state system. From there it expanded upward and outward into cooperative efforts with four-year colleges and university centers, and into the bordering tri-state area. Soon the ramifications of this form of organization expanded into the multistate scene through the formation of the national AACJC consortium. The dynamic potential of international education can knit students and faculty constituencies across all age groups and geographical boundaries.

Second, an international dimension can bring national attention to colleges working with youth in the thirteenth and fourteenth year of education. This population, thought to be exclusively concerned with local and regional matters, had not been regarded as visible on the national scene nor as possessing an international dimension. But it has been shown that the latent international interest, when supported by the cooperative force of the institutions housing this young population, can have a substantial potential for visibility and power.

The development of international dimensions at Rockland has demonstrated how the format of the interinstitutional consortium can have a direct influence on national policy making for this educational sector. Thus, promotion of an international dimension through a consortium-type organization has enabled faculties of community colleges to enrich their own academic lives and interests, gain national impact, and earn local recognition for seeking new horizons.

5. The College Consortium for International Studies

In the foregoing chapter, the International/Intercultural Consortium was described. The I/IC is a national consortium concerned with multiple aspects of international education and sponsored by a national organization, the AACJC.

The I/IC, important as it has become as an expression of nationwide concern about international education for community colleges, does not sponsor or conduct a single program overseas. Since it exists under the aegis of a national organization, it is unable to offer academic programs abroad or, for that matter, teach any courses or grant academic credits. The Consortium is extremely helpful, though, as a unifying force, and serves its purpose of introducing the concept of international education into the community college.

The I/IC was created by a number of innovative community colleges and farsighted individuals on the national scene and was helped into existence by certain organizations, one of which was the Tri-State Consortium. The

International/Intercultural Consortium expanded over the years as a national organization with a strong mission and a solid form, but without content.

Such content was introduced on a nationwide basis through the creation of a new organization that fused form with content in a viable manner. The College Consortium for International Studies (CCIS) was created in 1976 as a direct outgrowth of the Tri-State Consortium. As membership applications to the original consortium in the three states grew, as programs and the student population abroad multiplied, and as more colleges in other states expressed a desire to join, the time came to expand the Tri-State Consortium into the College Consortium.

While the Tri-State Consortium at best assisted the I/IC into existence, it was definitely the parent organization for the newly created College Consortium.

The CCIS is an umbrella organization encompassing the overseas academic programs of all member colleges. These programs, begun so tentatively in a single community college and later enlarged and multiplied through the multistate consortium, were now assured continuity through an ongoing organization of colleges from across the nation. Perpetuation of international educational programs was insured by the new nationwide consortium.

PURPOSE OF CCIS

The new consortium differs substantially from other consortia organized along the same lines. The main points of contrast are as follows:

1. The CCIS is a single-purpose organization providing high-quality international programs abroad for students enrolled in member colleges and universities. While the Consortium is strongly committed to all aspects of international education, and recognizes the important roles of area studies, foreign languages, international curricula, and so on, its single mission is the creation and maintenance of overseas programs for students and faculty.

2. The Consortium offers these programs without distinction to the total range of the student population, from entering freshmen to graduating seniors. While some courses of study may have academic prerequisites that may prevent freshmen from participating, the CCIS "is founded on the belief that international/intercultural experiences are integral to the education of all students—freshmen, sophomores, juniors and seniors."[1]

3. In order to accommodate the whole range of undergraduates, the original community-college (Tri-State) consortium had to be enlarged vertically as well as horizontally to encompass, in addition, four-year colleges and universities. Thus, the CCIS now lists among its membership many types of institutions of higher education, such as specialized colleges, universities, community colleges, and four-year institutions.

4. The types of programs offered overseas are different from the standard single-program, regular Junior Year Abroad experience. The CCIS approach is a holistic one, with the "overseas studies program . . . designed according to the philosophy: 'Let the country be the curriculum.' Using all of the educational resources of each country, CCIS programs provide students with meaningful intercultural academic learning experiences."[2] Although that goal has not yet been reached in all the countries where the Consortium offers study opportunities, the wide variety of programs conducted—for example, in Israel (described in detail in Chapter 3)—bear testimony to the

philosophical commitment. The thrust of program development is definitely in the direction of the statement quoted above.

5. The CCIS sponsors only semester- or year-long programs abroad; all short-term programs overseas are conducted by individual member colleges. Thus, consortium colleges can recruit and accommodate students from other colleges in their short-term course offerings, while official CCIS sponsorship is reserved for the semester and yearly programs.

6. The Consortium does not consider fluency in a foreign language to be a prerequisite for study in another country. While the CCIS strongly advocates the study of other languages and requires its students overseas to enroll in language courses in those countries where English is not spoken, the absence of foreign-language fluency should not prevent a student from participation in a meaningful academic program and intercultural experience overseas. Accordingly, the CCIS will offer to its student population "a wide spectrum of programs designed to accommodate the needs of students ranging from those with little or no knowledge of a country and/or its language to students familiar with the country and/or fluent in its language."[3]

7. The Consortium will furnish each student in a CCIS sponsored program overseas with American college credits for the work done abroad, provided the student fulfills the academic requirements and receives a passing grade for the courses he or she is enrolled in. Each student must be registered at an American member institution prior to departure, with that institution providing the academic transcripts and credits upon his or her return to this country. The student is thus spared the problem of having to translate the academic work done abroad into

American college credits while continuing his studies in the United States after his return from the foreign country and institution.

8. The Consortium has established a procedure according to which all CCIS sponsored semester/yearly programs become the property of each member institution. The colleges and universities that comprise the Consortium, therefore, can offer all available CCIS study possibilities overseas as their *own* programs to their student population and faculty. In this way the Consortium spares its member colleges the considerable expense of developing separate programs overseas without usurping the autonomy of the individual institutions. By offering a complete set of ready-made study-abroad possibilities to all members, the Consortium can "help conserve limited institutional resources through cooperative efforts."[4]

9. The organization has attached "culture components" to its program offerings in the various countries. Whether a student studies the German language in Heidelberg, Shakespeare in London and Stratford, or art history in Florence, at least one required course is devoted to the student's immersion in the culture of the country in which he or she is spending time. Thus, students enrolled in CCIS programs overseas will not be in classrooms only, but are exposed to intercultural experiences as well. In one of these culture-components courses (for example, Colloquium on British Culture), students travel every other weekend to historically or culturally important sites under the guidance of British instructors. These study trips are supplemented by academic lectures during the preceding week on subjects related to the places visited.

10. The CCIS plays an important role in faculty development for all member colleges through the sponsorship of faculty seminars overseas. These seminars are frequently financially supported by host countries or institutions abroad. They are designed to familiarize faculty members with foreign institutions, research projects, or scientific advances in their respective disciplines. While introducing the faculty to new projects or different methods abroad, participation in these seminars abroad also adds considerable international consciousness and global vision to their perspective. Most member colleges have made some financial contributions to enable their own faculty members to participate in these seminars.

Considering all ten points, it is easy to see that CCIS has indeed succeeded in creating a national organization unique in its offerings, flexible enough to accommodate varied institutions, and determined to provide the student population and faculty of its member colleges with quality academic and intercultural experiences in foreign countries.

ORGANIZATION OF CCIS

A most significant aspect of the viability of this Consortium rests in its structure and organization. Although developed along traditional organizational lines, it is designed specifically to serve the goals of the CCIS. Since 1976, the Consortium has worked relatively smoothly and seems to have matured through time.

At the heart of the organization is "a Board of Directors which shall be composed of the Presidents of the participating institutions."[5] The chairperson "and such other officers as the Board shall deem appropriate"[6] are elected by the membership. The function of the Board of Directors is twofold: (1) to establish policies and guidelines for the CCIS, and (2) to "annually establish the institutional membership fee."[7] The Board of Directors meets at least once annually at the CCIS office in New York City.

The organizational body charged with the actual day-to-day operation of the CCIS is the Executive Committee. This Executive Committee consists of nine institutional members and the executive director of the Consortium, of which "six are representatives of sponsoring institutions and three of member but non-sponsoring institutions."[8] The Executive Committee is "elected for a three-year term by a majority vote of the general membership in attendance at the spring general meeting. Institutions not elected to membership on the Executive Committee are entitled to designate a non-voting observer to the Committee."[9]

The permanent executive director of the Consortium is "elected by a majority vote of the Executive Committee for a three-year term."[10] It is the function of this ten-member Executive Committee to implement the policies and guidelines established by the Board of Directors of the Consortium. In addition, the Committee is responsible for

1. the orderly operation of the CCIS;
2. conducting the business activities;
3. reviewing existing and proposed programs; and
4. the creation of subcommittees as the need arises.

There are two officers of the Executive Committee—the chairperson and secretary—elected during the general June meeting; both serve for a two-year period.

The duties and functions of the permanent executive director are:

1. to facilitate communication and cooperation among and between member colleges;

2. to issue a bi-monthly newsletter to CCIS members;
3. to serve as Treasurer of the CCIS and prepare an annual financial report;
4. to schedule all regular meetings of the Executive Committee;
5. to call special meetings of the Executive Committee as the need arises; and
6. to keep the records of the CCIS.[11]

All meetings of the CCIS operate according to *Robert's Rules of Order,* with a quorum consisting of five persons. Executive Committee members who are unable to attend a scheduled meeting may assign their vote to another member or send a replacement to the meeting.

"Each member of the Executive Committee shall be entitled to one vote, with the exception of the Permanent Executive Director, who shall vote only in case of a tie."[12]

During Executive Committee meetings, a simple majority of elected members present is sufficient to take action.

Finally, the minutes of all Executive Committee meetings are mailed to all member institutions of the CCIS.

PROGRAM POLICIES

The structure of the Consortium has now been fully presented. It remains to be explained how the organization functions and how its policies are put into actual operation. The guiding principle in the operation of the CCIS is to maintain the continuing interest of the participating colleges, to enlarge the membership of the Consortium, and to offer flexible and adaptable academic programs overseas to an ever-increasing number of students in the participating colleges.

In order to achieve these ends, a number of specific policies guiding the creation and maintenance of overseas programs had to be accepted and enacted by the general membership. These program policies regulate the rights and responsibilities of all member institutions in the operation of or participation in overseas programs. They are set forth in detail below:

1. All program proposals for new and additional programs are to be submitted to the Executive Committee of the CCIS. Only member colleges may propose programs.

2. Any member college that has initiated a program and is conducting it successfully overseas has the first right to that program. If, however, this college decides not to conduct a program of which it is in charge, another member college may do so.

3. Any college in the CCIS may initiate a program overseas as long as it does not duplicate one already in existence.

4. All program proposals are to be submitted to the Executive Committee for approval; however, only those programs approved by the Committee will be designated as "CCIS programs."

5. Any program proposal submitted by a CCIS member college to the Executive Committee will have to be subjected by that college to the same screening procedures as any other on-campus program or course.

6. Any student enrolled in a CCIS member college who wants to enroll in any CCIS academic program overseas should register for that program on his home campus, even if the program abroad is conducted by another college in the CCIS.

7. Most importantly, the "CCIS member college collecting the tuition for a program must recognize that program as part of its curriculum and provide the academic credits"[13] for the student enrolled in that program.

8. The college in charge of a program overseas has the responsibility of evaluating the academic performance of any student enrolled in the program, regardless of the home campus at which the student is enrolled. This college also must forward the grades earned by that student to his or her home campus.

9. A CCIS college conducting a semester program overseas has the right to set and enforce the admissions standards and any other selection criteria it sees fit to establish.

10. In accordance with these program policies, a college in charge of a study-abroad program has the responsibility to provide all necessary academic and other support services to all students enrolled in the program during their study period overseas.

11. Any membership college of the CCIS has the right to on-site inspection and evaluation of any CCIS sponsored program. Designated faculty members or administrators are eligible to conduct these reviews overseas.

12. All member colleges of the Consortium must publicize *all* CCIS approved overseas academic programs. Only the Executive Committee can waive this stipulation, and only in unusual circumstances.

13. Using a format prescribed by the Executive Committee, information on all approved CCIS programs will be distributed to all membership colleges.

14. Any college in charge of a program overseas must notify the CCIS office at a special date of its intention not to offer the program during the following academic year. If more than one institution should be interested in taking over that program, the CCIS Executive Committee shall decide the issue of competing claims.

15. Evaluations of students and of "CCIS programs are mandatory; member colleges will develop their own method of evaluation in cooperation with the CCIS Executive Committee. The results of these evaluations will be made available to member colleges of the CCIS upon request."[14]

Once the program policies were established, the types of programs offered by the Consortium had to be specifically delineated.

TYPES OF CONSORTIUM PROGRAMS

The cross-cultural emphasis is paramount in all CCIS programs overseas and has a most desirable impact on the various programs offered. Three types of study programs are offered by the CCIS.

By far the majority of CCIS approved programs overseas are formal, structured classroom programs and are usually attached to institutions of higher learning in the host country. The program lasts for one semester (or a year) and involves 15–30 academic credits and enrollment in five college courses per semester. These courses are taught by foreign faculty members and are on topics that are especially relevant to the country in which the student is studying. The program is designed to supplement and enrich the student's chosen major academic field and provide him with choices that he would not have on his home campus. The semester program overseas is arranged before the student's departures by the CCIS affiliated college and the university abroad. The Consortium maintains close relationships wtih the overseas institutions. Subject areas range from the humanities and liberal arts to more specialized fields such as criminal justice and business administration.

A second category of semester program offerings consists of the "service learning" experience. Service learning is the "attempt to fuse two approaches to learning: learning through experience and learning from a mentor. The teacher acts as a mentor who helps each student design a learning program whose core is the experience of community service."[15] Thus, service learning provides an alternative "experience for those who wish to combine classroom instruction with the opportunity to serve and work."[16]

A third type of program offered overseas to students enrolled in CCIS member colleges is the "contract/independent study" method. A student "studying independently enters into a contractual arrangement with a mentor representing the CCIS institution of his choice."[17] The student, either by himself or under the guidance of his mentor, has to identify very specific objectives for the learning contract and the activities through which these objectives must be achieved. The methods of evaluation and all other contract components are entered into prior to the departure of the student for his overseas study program. The signed contract can be modified or altered only through an agreement between the student and the mentor. Contract study, "particularly overseas, is a very rigorous academic undertaking that requires imagination, self-discipline, planning and foresight in addition to the usual qualities of a good student."[18]

ASPECTS OF ADMINISTRATION

Only a smoothly working administration can overcome the difficulties that usually accompany international education programs involving large numbers of students. Choices of admission, matters of recordation, the adjustment of academic credits and their transfer to the home campus have to be worked out in an interinstitutional pattern. Most importantly, the financial arrangements between the home colleges, which collect tuition payments, and the institutions abroad that provide instructional services must be streamlined so as not to jeopardize the students' overseas experience. The CCIS addressed these administrative questions and has developed a very successful model.

The admission policy of the CCIS states that member colleges and universities should be able to offer to all eligible students an opportunity to pursue part of their college education outside the United States. Students wishing to enroll in programs overseas apply to the admissions office at the CCIS college or university nearest their place of residence. The evaluation of students who want to study abroad is based on their academic ability, maturity, motivation, and potential adaptability to a foreign culture. The specific admissions requirements for individual programs are determined by the member colleges conducting the program overseas.

After admission to a program, students register at one of the member colleges or universities in the United States and pay the appropriate tuition to the institution. In many cases, payment of the home-campus tuition covers all *instructional* costs abroad. In those cases where the instructional costs overseas exceed the payment the home campus can make toward them, a student is assessed a small surcharge to cover the difference between his home campus's instructional payment to the foreign institution and the actual cost of the program abroad.

While overseas, all CCIS students are monitored

through CCIS-affiliated offices or individual mentors. Upon successful completion of the formal program or after fulfillment of the learning contract, each student will receive an academic transcript from the CCIS member college at which he or she registered, which lists the grades achieved or the course equivalence of the work done through the contract agreement. This procedure greatly facilitates transfer of academic credits to other United States institutions after the student's return from a program overseas.

The CCIS has become the only nationwide organization that offers a large variety of overseas academic programs for community-college students from different states. While some two-year institutions and perhaps even some consortia still maintain independent programs, most community-college students study overseas under the aegis of CCIS, which is able to attract colleges and students because of its efficient organization and functioning.

Colleges also turn to CCIS because of its longstanding reputation. Its stability reassures colleges that do not have the expertise themselves to provide academically viable programs abroad for their students. The Consortium's experience of several years offers newcomers needed guidance. As individual colleges are less able to mount such ventures single-handedly, particularly during times of financial constraints, the CCIS continues to act as a focus through which such efforts may be channeled.

In addition to successfully placing students abroad, CCIS has facilitated the cooperation of community and four-year colleges in international education. This has signaled a new unification within American higher education. As a minor triumph, a modus operandi that originated within community colleges for the benefit of its students alone has now encompassed four-year colleges and universities as well. The organizational procedures developed have been adopted by upper-division institutions to send their own freshmen and sophomores abroad; thus, community colleges, which owe much to their older sister institutions, have been able to enrich those colleges and universities in turn.

6. Overseas Academic Programs — Administrative Support Systems

Development of an international program at any community college is possible only through outreach. But successful interinstitutional cooperation cannot take place without strong internal administrative organization. This chapter lists the various agencies, on and off campus, whose support is necessary in order to make international programs an ongoing, all-campus and community activity.

There are three major areas of interest here: the central administration of a college, the on-campus student support services, and the external, off-campus entities. The inclusion of all three illustrates the extent to which the administration of international programs will cut across all segments of on- and off-campus college relations. It is a sign of success and a measure of understanding if the local program administrator can work equally well with all three. More importantly, he or she has to be able to elicit ongoing support from these three segments in order to have continuously successful programs.

CENTRAL CAMPUS ADMINISTRATION

Ideally, the complete support and total cooperation of all major administrative offices as well as the top administrators on a college campus is needed for a program to be truly successful. Since it is unrealistic to expect such an ideal situation, it is important for the person in charge of international programs to single out those administrators without whose support the venture simply cannot succeed.

The central figure, as was pointed out above, will always be the president of the college, whose full support is needed to make the achievement of the stated objectives possible. The president's concern and support must be an almost perfect balance between letting the program director operate on his own and giving active support when help and cooperation are really needed. It is this balance that is largely responsible for the successful interplay between the chief administrative office of the college and the person responsible for the international components. The outcome of the venture is a direct result of the success in achieving this balance.

If a president has a firm commitment to international education, this commitment will be known and understood on campus and most of the immediately subordinate officers will demonstrate a willingness to cooperate. The readiness of a president to support the program will filter down to the college vice-presidents and deans. This vertical "ripple effect" will mean that the international staff will receive support from central college administration, even during the absence of the president from the campus. Thus the program will be uninterrupted. As a president gains stature from his increasingly visible efforts on behalf of international education on and off campus, his influence will be enhanced because of his success in bringing a new dimension—international education—to his college.

A second effect will be horizontal. As vice-presidents and deans leave the institution to assume administrative posts in other colleges and state agencies, they will take with them the international commitment they acquired while on campus. They will have accepted the idea of international dimensions in community colleges, and, more practically, they will take along the knowledge that such programs are indeed possible.

Particularly in the very early stages, the president's position and power is the major means of removing bottlenecks and cutting across administrative and bureaucratic barriers. In the absence of guidelines and precedents for an overseas program, it cannot become successful without determination and assistance of the president of the college. As time goes on, he must maintain his support, even though the college will have accepted international programs and his direct participation may no longer be necessary. His vision and imagination must continue in order to stretch the horizons of the college and the capacities of his DIE.

Any international office operates on a variety of different levels, such as the faculty, administrative, student, and community levels, and cuts across various on- and off-campus segments. The operation does not easily fit into the usual bureaucratic structure of educational institutions, and the Office of International Education, therefore, needs an operational style that depends on the ability to work on many different levels and elicit support from various quarters.

As indicated above, the success of the OIE at any community college depends on the selection of its director. He or she must share the vision of the president of the

college as well as possess the administrative skill to operate the program.

In addition, the ability to work closely with the faculty
is extremely helpful, since it will be virtually impossible
to mount programs successfully without their support. It
is for that reason that most DIEs are recruited from the
faculty.

It should be noted that it is not easy to design a successful OIE on a community-college campus. While the
various components that make up such an office can be
listed, experience has shown that a successful OIE evolves
usually over a period of years and is greatly influenced by
institutional commitments and financial constraints.

In the beginning, a faculty member, usually on an overtime basis, will undertake to create a few overseas academic programs in addition to his teaching duties. As the
need arises, part-time secretarial staff may be added. It is
usually difficult to justify the creation of an OIE and the
appointment of a full-time director from the very start for
the sole purposes of adding an international dimension to
a community college. In the beginning, these tasks can be
achieved in addition to regular teaching duties by a competent faculty member.

Various campus offices must be contacted in order to
develop and harmonize international programs. The Offices of the Registrar, Records, and Admissions are most
important. The registrar must develop a mechanism for
transfer of course credits abroad to a student's transcript.
A new method is needed to replace the old way in which
each course taken by a student abroad must be equated
to a similar course listed in the home campus catalog so
that appropriate college credits can be assigned.

A student frequently takes a course or a program
abroad because similar courses simply are not offered at

the American college. Obviously, one of the purposes of overseas academic programming is the exposure of students to courses that are not available on their home campuses. Thus, a program in Denmark may offer courses such as Nordic mythology, Scandinavian history, or Danish design, which will not be part of a regular community-college curriculum in this country.

The new method of recording suggested above achieves a flexibility that permits the enrichment of community-college programs by unusual courses abroad. With this new procedure, it should be possible to accept a full one-semester, fifteen-credit program and transfer it to the home campus as fifteen academic credits taken at the University of Y in country X, with the individual courses simply listed, one to five. Although these courses do not appear in the college catalog, the home campus should accept responsibility for the fifteen credits, thereby enabling the student to transfer the package together with the other courses taken at the home campus to the college of his choice after graduation from the community college.

The records office, working in close cooperation with the registrar's office, should also develop methods for easier transfer of grades and credits for courses taken in foreign institutions. This is absolutely essential. Many overseas academic programs have students studying at foreign institutions where the instructors are not part of a regular American college faculty and thus do not assign American-type college credits. The students, however, are Americans, who have paid regular tuition to their home college prior to departure and, therefore, require their regular examinations and grades to be translated into academic credits.

Without the assistance and cooperation of the records office, it will not be possible to translate overseas course evaluations and grades onto home college transcripts. Thus, the advantage of having foreign courses appear on the students' community-college transcripts will have been lost.

New procedures can be developed so that such course listings, titles, numbers, credits, and grades are easy to transfer. Several two-year institutions have successfully adopted new models so that student achievements in the international programs can be preserved on home-campus transcripts.

While the registrar's office and the records office adapt their procedures to help facilitate international programs, the admissions office must respond in kind. When more and more students start to enroll in community colleges to participate in overseas academic programs, it will be necessary for the admissions office to adjust to changing conditions and a new clientele. New forms and procedures will have to be developed and introduced to streamline the process by which a student can transfer to a college for one semester only and then return to his home campus after the semester abroad.

The regular admissions procedure for a student who stays on the community-college campus for the full two years is usually cumbersome compared to the shorter procedure for those who enroll only for the purpose of spending one semester in a program abroad. By using more simplified forms, it is possible for students to participate in overseas study programs with a minimum of bureaucratic red tape.

The Offices of the Registrar, Records, and Admissions must work harmoniously with the top administration of the college to ease entry into overseas academic programs, record procedures, and transfer credits. This cooperative response demonstrates how the goals of central college

administration can be translated into the removal of bureaucratic barriers within the college. Top administration's commitment to international programs thus serves
to break down the usual resistance to new procedures, and
the programs themselves are the ultimate beneficiaries of
that breakdown.

In order to achieve the full benefit and success of international programs, the college libraries and their staffs
must be involved actively in amassing international reference material. Development of a reference library on international education for students, faculty, and administrators may take a number of years. The library must also
obtain audiovisual materials such as films, video tapes, and
slides. Since this is an ongoing process, the international
education reference library and audiovisual collection will
reach full strength only over a period of time. Cooperation
of the library staff must be complete, and funds for these
new materials should be set aside in the library budget
from the very beginning of the project.

The success of the entire international program rests on
the allocation of an adequate budget. With few exceptions,
all budgetary support for the project must be carried by
the college, at least in the early stages. All academic programs have to be treated financially according to guidelines developed and enforced by the appropriate state education department. Thus, if overseas academic programs
can be treated *as if* these programs are conducted on
campus, then a major roadblock for the adequate financing of the venture is removed. It has to be pointed out
that the community-college conducting the program overseas awards the academic credits to its students enrolled
in it. It is, therefore, only logical to assume that the
courses offered in the program are regular college courses

regardless of whether these courses are conducted on campus, off campus, in another city or overseas. Appropriate financial support for the instruction of the students abroad should be made available from the home-campus budget.

ON-CAMPUS STUDENT SUPPORT SERVICES

Central administration support and actions described so far need to be supplemented by an account of on-campus student services. First, the role of the dean of students and his staff is of utmost importance.

The dean's office is particularly significant because of its central role on campus and even abroad. From the start, the dean and his staff must personally provide vital cooperation, support, and understanding of the goals of the venture. This effort will manifest itself on two levels: First, student personnel services have to be made available to those students intending to enroll in international programs. In fact, the Office of the Dean can and should be especially helpful in counseling students into the program and monitoring them while abroad. Second, the Office of the Dean of Students should evaluate overseas academic programs through personal interviews, visits, and follow-up questionnaires. Ideally, the dean and his staff should design a comprehensive set of provisions for an appropriate international education component in the whole student personnel service area.

Any student applying at a community college should be made aware, from the moment first contact is made, that he is entering a college committed to international education and with a keen awareness of the responsibility to bring the world to the campus. This commitment can be demonstrated in a variety of ways through student personnel services.

For example, students should be informed of the complete range of overseas studies programs available at the college when requesting information or assistance from counselors. During freshman week, a one-week orientation program designed to familiarize entering freshmen with college life, the dean of students can provide a member of the OIE with the opportunity to meet with the entering freshman class to explain and discuss the overseas education programs available at the college. Subsequently, the OIE representative may meet with interested students on a one-to-one basis or in small groups for further questions and continuing explorations.

This procedure provides entering freshmen with an opportunity to familiarize themselves with all international programs and overseas study opportunities available to them. If interested, these students can then structure their curriculum accordingly, that is, they can plan a one-semester program abroad into their academic career at the college from the very beginning. It should be kept in mind that careful planning for overseas academic programs is a necessity, since students in a community college stay on campus an average of only two years. The semester most appropriate for an overseas experience is the third semester, the beginning of the sophomore year. These orientation meetings with entering freshmen can turn out to be most helpful to students as well as rewarding to the OIE.

Another form of assistance by the dean of students is the assignment of one counselor as a liaison person between the OIE and dean of students. That counselor, in addition to keeping the two offices informed about new developments, should work in close cooperation with the OIE and become involved in the activities of that office.

For example, as a member of the Office of the Dean of Students it is possible for him to determine whether a prospective candidate for programs overseas had any previous involvement with drugs, should there be a notification on the student's record. In addition, he can involve himself in all questions of credit transfer on behalf of either the student or the college. When problems arise about transferability of academic credits abroad, he can clear up those questions more easily prior to the student's departure for the program overseas. Also, he should be actively involved in counseling prospective students as well as those actually participating in overseas academic programs. Finally, the counselor should monitor students while abroad. Questions of deadlines, forms, and application procedure to other colleges need constant attention.

In summary, the various personnel services are in a position to make more than adequate provisions to incorporate an international education component into their own activities. These services can help to ensure a more thorough inclusion of the new venture into the regular college routine.

A second important role can be played by the Office of the Dean of Students as evaluator of overseas programs. The dean may accompany a group of students overseas or visit them while they are abroad. Upon his return to the campus, he or she will then be able to write an external evaluative report on nonacademic matters such as logistics, student behavior, emergency cases, and scheduling of student interaction with the local population. In addition, the Office of the Dean of Students should routinely conduct follow-up evaluations of these programs through questionnaires and personal interviews of returning students.

In no way, however, should these evaluative procedures on the general conduct of overseas programs be left to the campus OIE. This office should not pass judgment on its own programs. Academic questions and course evaluations are obviously within the province of the Office of the Academic Dean.

Over time, any community college conducting overseas academic programs should develop and have available a comprehensive picture of its activities abroad. This picture will become necessary when the college contemplates an enlargement of the program. Successful justification of existing programs almost inevitably will make the inauguration of future programs easier.

One method of developing such a comprehensive picture is the practice of one-to-one discussions between a student who has just returned from overseas and a professional counselor attached to the Office of the Dean of Students. This counselor should be intimately familiar with the program under discussion and, in addition, must have a good working knowledge of overseas academic programs generally. The counselor designated to work with the OIE would be the most logical choice for these interviews.

If the program is truly successful, the single student interview procedure may not work well owing to the large numbers of students involved. In this case, only those students who have been abroad at least a semester should be considered for personal interviews. Perhaps the evaluation of short-term programs then could be left largely to the departments that are academically involved in them and to faculty members and supervisory administrative personnel who conduct these programs abroad. There should be, then, two types of person-to-person evaluations: by the student counselor for long-term programs and by others for short-term programs.

According to counselor evaluations conducted at a number of community colleges running successful overseas academic programs, perhaps the most important and most observable impact of student exposure to international programs has been the increased maturity shown by these students upon their return to the college community. This maturity is evident not only in their personal relationships and objectives but also in their job performance in vocational areas.

The semester and year-long programs have been extremely important to the social awareness of students. Faculty members who have visited and evaluated community-college programs overseas have drawn similar conclusions.

In addition, most students who have been away from their campus for a semester or longer demonstrate their international awareness through participation in various curricular and extracurricular activities during subsequent semesters on campus. Unfortunately, very few colleges have attempted to utilize the resources these students bring back to the campus community in any constructive or institutionalized way.

Short-term programs, according to questionnaires and person-to-person interviews, have provided the following benefits: For the majority of community-college students, whose academic careers terminate with the two-year degree, the short overseas academic program was the only means of ever studying abroad or spending a short period of time overseas (with an academic component attached to the experience) before entering the job market. These programs duplicate for the community-college student, on a reduced scale, the Junior Year Abroad experience, which was and still is a significant component of a student's education during a regular four-year college career.

The space allocated here to the work of the Office of the Dean of Students reflects the importance of this Office in helping to carry out international plans and programs at a community college. The Financial Aid Office is also relevant for community-college students who want to study overseas. This office must be helpful and cooperative from the beginning for the whole project to be successful. All international programs should be treated by the Financial Aid Officer as regular college course offerings to compete with on-campus courses and programs on an equal basis; all financial aid, whether loans, scholarships, grants, federal or state aid, should be fully applicable and available to students participating in international education programs abroad.

The fact that all overseas academic programs are offered for academic credits makes it possible to offer financial aid to students participating in these programs. Ideally, the Financial Aid Office should make a special effort to assist students going overseas, perhaps even on a priority basis, since these students' financial need exceeds that of students who study on campus only.

Another major feature of introducing international dimensions into a community college could be the establishment of an international component on campus, perhaps a separate unit within the college along the cluster-college principle. It should develop its own curriculum, recruit its own student population, set up its own degree guidelines and programs, and serve as a feeder unit for overseas academic programs.

The establishment of such a cluster college would result

in increased international interest, activities, and competence of the faculty. In addition to broadening curricular offerings in the international field, it would also have its own faculty bent on enlarging the international dimensions at the college.

Since overseas academic programs are selective by nature, this cluster college could address itself specifically to the needs of those students interested in international education but unable to participate in overseas academic programs for financial or other reasons. It would serve as an anchor for overseas programs on the home campus designed to develop a strong, campuswide interest in international education. Students graduating from this cluster college could then feed into international offerings of wider and more varied scope at other colleges. The degree-program curriculum, ideally, should prescribe that the first semester be spent on campus with a strong foreign-area concentration, to be followed by a second semester largely spent with a subculture in the community at large. The third semester would be spent abroad in the geographical area of the student's concentration, and the final semester on the home campus again.

The creation of such a cluster college on campus will further the development of international activities in a community college, and the academic curriculum will have to keep pace. As a matter of fact, an increased international focus on campus cannot succeed without a corresponding increase in international curricular offerings.

OFF-CAMPUS SUPPORT AGENCIES

To be completely successful in internationalizing a community college, a college must seek every possible

area of support. This effort should reach for on-campus
and off-campus involvement. A variety of forces can be
brought into play to solidify achievements of overseas college programs. Community participation, the public media,
and relations with industry, commerce, and the arts can
all contribute to the success of these programs. Suggestions are given here for ways in which off-campus support
can play an important part in maintaining the momentum
of overseas education programs in community colleges.

All international on-campus events, such as workshops,
speakers, and lectures sponsored by the college and designed to internationalize the campus, must be opened to
the community at large. Serious attempts should be made
to attract and involve the community in these events on
campus. If some of these offerings are of particular interest to special segments in the community, perhaps the
campus division of continuing education can make a
particular effort to contact these community groups.

Educational institutions in the area, to provide just one
example, should be notified if well-known educators visit
the college for special lectures on international/intercul-
tural education topics. During such events, attendance by
high school teachers and members of the community is to
be strongly encouraged.

In addition, off-campus professional community groups,
such as lawyers or doctors, can be made aware through
their elected representatives (AMA, Bar Association) of
international professional meetings and congresses. The
college can ask professional associations if their members
are particularly interested in attending similar meetings
abroad. If sufficient support is demonstrated, the college
can offer as a community service to assist in facilitating attendance at these events.

One specific example may suffice. The Worldwide

Congress of Pediatricians was held in 1977 in New Delhi, India. At least one community college, through its division of continuing education, established contact with the local association of pediatricians. The college offered to make all necessary arrangements for the group of pediatricians, thereby demonstrating its interest in community service. While making the arrangements, special requests by the group were taken into consideration. The members wanted to make an interim stop in London for additional meetings with colleagues and to attend a series of lectures by out-standing British pediatricians. The community college, through its contacts in London and with the help of a number of agencies there, was in a position to structure the London add-on accordingly. Efforts to draw profes-sional groups into the community college constitute one more mechanism for successful community outreach while attempting to internationalize the college and the com-munity.

Another attempt to reach into the community can be made through the use of the public media. The local com-munity should be kept informed of all international edu-cation programs sponsored by the community college. Through the use of newspaper stories, perhaps best writ-ten by past program participants, the community in gen-eral receives a vivid picture of the variety of activities of-fered abroad, while getting a first-hand report on their academic quality. Radio interview programs, usually con-ducted by local radio stations, can be asked to invite stu-dents who have returned from one of the semester or yearly overseas academic programs. Some of these radio programs allow listeners to phone in questions to the an-nouncer, who will discuss these questions with partici-pants. On these types of programs, perhaps a member of the campus OIE may be asked to participate to respond with knowledgeable answers to phoned-in questions. Experience at some community colleges has shown that while a few of the questions on programs of this kind are critical, mainly in the area of budget, taxes, and public expenditures, the vast majority of the calls and inquiries have been highly favorable and laudatory. Many of the critical questions are based on ignorance, since no college budget funds support the travel or room and board of students abroad. Participants in these programs always have to supply those funds themselves. Local radio stations also may be asked to run a series of broadcasts on the various international activities conducted by the OIE both overseas and on the home campus.

Finally, all international programs and events should be continuously publicized throughout the college community, using display posters, the college journal, and local newspapers. A comprehensive brochure listing all overseas academic offerings should be available to any interested person upon request.

Another manner in which community colleges can reach into the local community is to contact interested groups when international education seminars are offered. School administrators, research scientists, and industrial groups may want to attend. Through the Division of Continuing Education, the needs of commerce and industry in the county can be brought to the attention of the international education specialists at the college for appropriate action or response.

Management seminars abroad are one more example of liaison with professional organizations and interested management specialists in the community. The Division of Continuing Education, in attempting to meet the needs of these industrial groups, can pass their requests for assistance in the international field on to the Office of International Education at the college. It would seem that the need always exists to strengthen the means by which the community can be made aware of the variety of programs and activities in international education available to students and the general community alike.

In conclusion, community colleges are becoming increasingly involved in international, technical and cultural cooperative projects. At a Conference on Funding for International Education conducted by the Center of International Programs, New York State Education Department, and held at the School of International Affairs, Columbia University, in 1976, the senior analyst, Office of Policy and Plans, Department of State, strongly suggested that, in comparison with large universities, community colleges are frequently better prepared to meet the educational needs in developing countries. He foresaw that government agencies would increasingly favor community colleges when funding international technical and cultural projects in the future. Local communities should be made aware immediately of any involvement of the community college in technical and/or cultural development projects. Knowledge of these projects will further reinforce the image of the college as being committed to adding a viable international dimension to its offerings.

Not all of the items or activities described in the preceding pages can be uniformly successful. Nonetheless, great support can be aroused, received, and filtered down through the entire organizational structure. Once the priorities for the college have been established and international commitments have been made, it is possible gradually to remove administrative obstacles and barriers, so that the venture can generate its own momentum. It is this momentum that will feed the ambition to expand the range of influence slowly beyond the campus. While the international activities within the international administrative context of the campus are usually crowned by success, off-campus involvements and projects sometimes remain unrealized. Nonetheless, they set the tone and mark the direction in which international programs on the community-college level should proceed.

7. Impact of International Programs on Faculty and Students

A decade of international activities at a community college must have a definite impact on students and faculty. But is such impact central or marginal? This chapter is an evaluation of the effectiveness of an international dimension on campus life in community colleges. Some of these colleges have made themselves nationally known, largely through the development of one specialty—the community-college international education dimension. What has been the effect of these activities internally?

First, originally reluctant faculty have often been turned around to become enthusiastic supporters. This support has become part of an established faculty profile that could be called "enlightened self-interest." Faculty members see benefits for themselves over and above the benefits to the community college, and they then become initiators as well as participants. They actively generate program development and then conduct short-term programs abroad.

Second, among the students, an almost total absence of international exposure is replaced by an increasingly large percentage of students taking part in overseas programs and participating in international activities on campus. In those community colleges that have become actively involved in international programs, the percentage of students participating in international activities abroad has varied between 5 and 18 percent of total enrollment. Internationalism has also had an effect on nonparticipating students, through the internationalization of the curriculum, foreign-language study, or involvement in on-campus international activities.

THE FACULTY

Owing to the nature of community colleges, their curriculum and general goals, the faculty usually does not possess the kind of broad international academic background found at universities offering graduate programs and engaging in a variety of research projects. However, community colleges usually have faculty members on their staff who bring to the campus at least some international interest, background, or experience and are, therefore, able to cooperate with the OIE on campus. Almost any community college, upon close scrutiny, will find a substantial number of faculty members who have some international background that can be utilized constructively by the college in its efforts to internationalize the campus. Most community colleges, however, are simply not aware of or have failed to make use of this potential.

For example, among the faculty members of a typical community college, 32 out of a permanent staff of 145 were found to have some international interest or background. Some were born abroad, some received academic training or degrees overseas, and other had already participated in overseas academic programs or were interested in specific world areas through their studies.

An increasing number of faculty members at some community colleges quickly gain international experience by participating in overseas academic course offerings. But these programs are not always conducted by faculty members who already have some international background. Most courses develop out of the academic departments (with the local OIE serving as catalyst). Many faculty members enjoy their first international experience through their participation in these courses. During the January intersession period, at least one community college, for example, has a total of eight to twelve faculty members in Western Europe every year. Mid-semester programs, summer workshops, and faculty seminars overseas are additional means to provide faculty members with a chance to gain exposure to foreign cultures and add some international interest and experience. This cross-cultural exposure of faculty members benefits the academic curriculum as well as the extracurricular activities on the home campus.

Faculty members often start to internationalize their curricular offerings after they return from program activities abroad. In addition, they involve themselves with greater frequency in international activities on campus, such as working with foreign students or participating in campus international days.

Institutional policies at internationally active community colleges have clearly favored foreign exposure of as many faculty members as possible. However, the number of students enrolled abroad has to be large enough to justify, financially and administratively, the necessity of sending a faculty member abroad.

Experience has demonstrated that in cases where community colleges have stationed faculty members overseas for longer periods (say, two years), these faculty members were ultimately replaced by local academicians. In other cases, foreign educational institutions served to coordinate the programs. This replacement policy can be cited as a definite improvement over the practice of many four-year institutions that continue to use home-campus faculty as teaching staff in their overseas programs. The whole purpose of overseas academic programming is called into question if students overseas are taught regular home-campus courses by home-campus faculty. Although it may be necessary to station a faculty member overseas to start up a program and check on the academic viability of the courses and curriculum, these program directors should be replaced by local faculty or administrators in due time. This replacement policy, in addition to improving the quality of most international programs, usually reduces the program cost of the sponsoring college as well.

Once a community college becomes significantly involved with overseas projects and establishes contacts with more and more agencies, organizations, and academic institutions abroad, the frequency of visits by foreign faculty members to the home campus will rapidly increase. This increase in the number of visiting foreign faculty will in turn contribute greatly to the growing awareness of international education activities on campus.

For example, twenty-six faculty members visited one community college during a three-year period after the introduction of international programs on that campus. They came either as guests of individual faculty members, as lecturers, or as visiting scholars and stayed from one day to a semester. The majority came from England and Israel, with the rest arriving from Germany, Denmark, India, Italy, and Yugoslavia. It may be relatively easy for a community college to invite foreign faculty members to the campus for a day, while they are on some exchange program or a study visit to this country financed by some other organization or foundation. The frequency with which foreign faculty members now visit community-college campuses and participate in seminars, lectures, and discussions with students and faculty is increasing each year. The fact that more and more community-college faculty members have spent time abroad while participating in or supervising overseas academic programs helps to increase the number of these visits. They are often an outgrowth of contacts established abroad.

The development of international competency among community-college faculty rests, at this stage, in the number of faculty members that can be successfully involved in overseas academic programs. By exposing more and more of them to other cultures (even though it might be for only a short time), new teaching patterns and other educational activities abroad will exert an influence. Not only those actively participating in the programs benefit but, in a larger sense, the faculty as a whole, and more importantly, the student population.

The internationalization of the faculty will permit the application of their services to the internal life of a college in new ways. This has become evident in two areas of campus life cited here. First, faculty counseling of students will receive a new impetus. Second, faculty participation on college committees will take on a new character through the creation of an international committee.

The academic advisory system of a community college should be made acutely aware of all overseas program offerings. All students enrolled or planning to enroll meet with a faculty member in an attempt to plan their academic programs for the following semester. If during the advisement period a student shows any interest in studying abroad, the faculty member may know of a suitable program, or should be able to direct the student to someone in a position to answer questions on overseas academic courses.

The development of international projects on community-college campuses usually results in or is preceded by the creation of a faculty committee. Such a committee serves as a linking mechanism on international education matters to the various academic departments and serves two functions: first, to feed back to the departments information on international education programs and then keep the faculty informed; second, and perhaps more importantly, to strengthen the relationship between the campus OIE and the departments, their chairpersons, and the faculty.

When the International Education Committee is being created at a community college, each academic department should nominate or elect one representative to meet with other committee members and a delegate from the Office of International Education at least once a month. They are to discuss, review, and evaluate matters and questions on international education generally and overseas programs specifically. Each committee member should be provided with time during the next meeting of his department to report back on the various activities, plans, and developments of international projects at the college.

It has been stated previously that no OIE on any community-college campus can function successfully without the active support and cooperation of the faculty, since most overseas programs develop out of the academic departments. Such has been the record so far of faculty participation in international activities at community colleges.

Three conclusions emerge: First, it is possible that some community colleges will take a different approach in the future and will grow internationally at different rates. Second, faculty members who want to participate actively in international activities on or off campus have to do so over and above their regular teaching duties. As these activities increase, however, teaching loads may be reduced accordingly. Third, efforts to internationalize the faculty over and above the ways described in the preceding pages are largely budgetary. It would involve the granting of leave for sabbaticals to study or develop courses abroad. In addition, perhaps, a more concerted effort could be made to consider international experience and interest as a crucial factor in the selection of new faculty. Since the faculty constitutes one of the major elements in the success or failure of international education activities on or off any community-college campus, the greatest possible support should be extended to those faculty members who already possess some international competency and to those who try to acquire international experience through sabbaticals or other activities abroad.

THE STUDENTS

The impact of student exposure to international education at community colleges has been increasingly significant over the years and can be divided into two areas, namely, on-campus and off-campus activities.

Immediate impact upon the student body occurs most often through the introduction of international programs on campus and the fallout effects of programs overseas. Not only is there a positive effect on students actually enrolled in programs overseas but these students in turn affect the student body as a whole. Other students on campus recognize, perhaps for the first time, that successful overseas programs can be conducted within a community-college curriculum and that an international component perhaps ought to be part of the total curriculum.

A second important international dimension on campus can be provided through the presence of foreign students.[1] These students are entering community colleges in ever-increasing numbers in spite of the fact that most of the institutions do not have dormitory facilities. The colleges, however, assist foreign students in securing living quarters with nearby families.

Most foreign students enrolled at a community college present a number of problems to the college, the major one being that of language. Also, many of the students, due to poor preparation in their home countries, have to go through a college skills program which teaches basic (noncredit) courses to entering freshmen. Another problem, further complicating the integration of foreign students, is that many of them enroll in satellite centers that are operated off campus by the community colleges. Since satellite centers usually do not have all of the educational facilities commonly available on main campuses (language labs, a sufficient number of counselors, library facilities, etc.), some of the foreign students in these centers may become lost. Community colleges are attempting to remedy this situation through early identification of foreign students in the admissions process and the assignment of more college skills and foreign language courses to satellite centers.

Most foreign students join the campus International Club, which provides fellowship to its members. These clubs may also sponsor international visits and nationality days, thus familiarizing the campus community with the home countries of the students through meetings, exhibitions of native crafts, films, and lectures. The clubs are mostly voluntary organizations, supported and perhaps partly financed by the local Student Senate. Foreign students frequently establish close contact and interact freely with ethnic groups in the community that are similar to their own.

Community colleges reflect, to some degree, the diversity of ethnic groups found in the community. These ethnic groups can be a valuable resource for the development of internationally innovative and culturally meaningful programs sponsored by the college. Representatives of ethnic-group associations or individuals may be invited to assist in the development of the curriculum for the international student group. Ethnic community groups may also provide help to students during ethnic heritage days on campus.

The presence and mix of ethnic and foreign students on a community-college campus adds strength to the aim of internationalizing the college and the local community. The support of both will contribute directly to the increasing awareness of American students of concepts such as cross-cultural contacts and international interdependence.

Cross-cultural workshops and conferences on campus also provide a means for introducing community-college students to the international scene. One community college, in cooperation with a number of other institutions, conducted a two-day workshop entitled "The Community College Looks to the 21st Century." This workshop was most successful and contributed significantly to the international education dimension in community colleges. The presentation of papers on international components in community colleges, lectures, and working sessions on curriculum imperatives, technical assistance, and study-abroad programs were part of the meetings. Most importantly, representatives of the federal government participating in the workshop became sensitized to the significance of community colleges in this area, and they, in turn, invited requests for the expansion of international education activities at this level of higher education.

Other community colleges over the years have developed a number of activities that are especially designed to introduce international elements into extracurricular campus offerings. Again, the purpose is to internationalize the campus and to make the students, the faculty, and the community aware of the various activities available to them in the international field.

These activities are usually made possible through the cooperation and financial assistance of the campus Office of Cultural Affairs. This office commonly serves as the administrative center for all cultural activities the community college sponsors, such as concerts, lectures, and theater or ballet performances, both on and off campus. The Office of Cultural Affairs, if active and imaginative, can be of great assistance in any attempt to internationalize a community college. Two examples may illustrate: At one community college, an international seminar is now sponsored on campus twice each academic year. Outstanding authorities in the field of international education are invited as visiting scholars to conduct a number of seminars, discussions, and orientation sessions for students, but with faculty and administrators participating. These international seminars have become a staple commodity at some community colleges, with interested faculty members bringing their classes to attend the meetings. Seminars such as these are one more vehicle for bringing an international dimension to the campus.

A second way in which the Office of Cultural Affairs can assist is by inviting special lecturers to the college. At some community colleges a number of outstanding speakers are invited during the academic year to present lectures and lead discussions with students and faculty on special international education topics. This speakers' program provides the OIE at the college with a chance to present well-known authorities to the general college population. The purpose of these lectures is twofold. First, they attract students to international topics so as to increase their awareness of international affairs and make them conscious of cross-cultural dimensions. Second, the lectures make the general student body aware of the international programs sponsored by the college through its OIE. The enhanced visibility of this office helps to maintain a high level of student enthusiasm for international activities on and off campus.

The impact of such international components in the extracurricular offerings at a community college are difficult to measure. Because of their variety, however, it can be safely assumed that they at least contribute to the goal of internationalizing the campus. Obviously, more could and perhaps should be done at these colleges toward that goal, but most of these activities are subject to budgetary restrictions and, therefore, certain limitations are placed on the number of extracurricular activities a college is able to offer in the field of international education. The activities just described are mostly for on-campus students of community-college age.

There are also off-campus activities that can be specifically designed to serve older students who often already have other academic qualifications but now may wish to add an international dimension to their lives. Frequently, these students are not interested in academic credits. Two examples demonstrate the possible scope and range of off-campus student activities at community colleges.

First, one community college offers a Performing Arts Workshop in London as one of its annual programs abroad. This workshop, open to nonstudents on an auditing basis, includes classes and lectures by playwrights, critics, actors, dancers, musicians, and directors, as well as backstage visits and attendance at experimental productions. It covers a wide range of activities in all areas of the performing arts. The workshop in London attracts a substantial number of nonstudent adults, making it possible for the college to reach out into the community while recognizing its responsibility to internationalize extracampus offerings. Obviously, there was a demand for this kind of program in the community, and the college responded accordingly. This program is now finding an ever-increasing number of imitators, as the transatlantic community in this field is constantly growing among community colleges.

Second, Divisions of Continuing Education at several community colleges conduct educational travel programs. These programs are designed for persons in the community who wish to travel under academic auspices but are not interested in college credits. Many community colleges have for years conducted similar programs *inside* the United States to historically important places such as Williamsburg, Virginia or Washington, D.C. Since these programs are usually developed as a community service, they do not carry academic credit. Generally, the academic content of the programs is not substantial enough to warrant the granting of credits. Several community colleges recognized that similar programs could be conducted abroad in subjects such as literature, art, music, and architecture. Because there is no language barrier, England is especially well suited for the establishment of such programs. Most of the participants in these programs have traveled to foreign countries before, but now they want to have their foreign experience supplemented by lectures, structured visits to museums, and seminars on special-interest topics.

As a result of these offerings, a whole new segment of the student population has been created at several community colleges.

In summary, the faculty and students at community colleges can be significantly affected by imaginative programs and activities provided to increase the level of international awareness. An initially disinterested faculty can be galvanized into international activity through the excitement of travel and foreign involvement. Eliciting faculty support depends on arousing enlightened self-interest, which in turn provides the fuel to propel these ventures on to success.

The inevitable bandwagon effect follows. Each successful program generates new suggestions and new programs. Once the support of the majority of the faculty has been secured, the creation of new programs—and often radically different programs such as in-service learning or contract studies abroad—can become a reality.

Turning to the student population, two things can happen. Various means can be utilized to elicit the interest and participation of the usual student population on campus. Off campus, a new student population can be created. The challenge is unending.

In spite of what has been achieved already, as demonstrated by the examples cited, there remains on the community-college campuses a segment of young students who are not aware of the presence of enriching foreign study opportunities. Existing programs are flexible enough within their current framework to make contact with this segment of the student population possible through new and innovative means.

The new off-campus student population reached through international programs, though radically different from the usual student body found on community-college campuses, can provide a new segment of strength and support for the college. The programs they demand are sometimes difficult to establish within the community-college setting. However, they are a beneficial challenge to faculty as well as to the college administration. The leadership of community colleges, in the pragmatic fashion of American education, must accept this challenge as an opportunity to enhance the educational offerings of the colleges. The new programs developed will in themselves expand their reach and influence. They once again prove that providing an international dimension to academic offerings will infuse new excitement into the college curriculum which in itself has pedagogical as well as substantive significance.

8. Review and Conclusions

Throughout this book an attempt has been made to provide an extensive description of how the international dimension at community colleges was conceived and developed. This description has carried implicit answers to the question of whether a community college should offer international training, to what extent it should do so, and how such training could be accomplished.

A number of broader questions have also been formulated. Is a community college, a self-contained single institution, enough of a locus for the establishment of international training, or should several colleges band together to combine the benefits of specialization with the power of the joint use of their resources? This book has also explored the wide-ranging impact of international exposure on the college and the college community as a whole.

The impact upon faculty, students, and surrounding community is of special significance, since community colleges have long been defined as narrow in scope, concerned only with local affairs, and conservative enough to fear the effects of international exposure.

135

Once the decision to introduce overseas academic programs into a community college is made, ways have been found to turn the idea into reality. Emotional commitment is the spark; from it administrative feasibility must be worked out.

This book has demonstrated how patient solution of administrative and financial problems is possible and that a commitment of public funds to international involvement can be secured. Doctrinal conviction alone cannot put an educational innovation into operation. Installation of satisfactory administrative and fiscal mechanisms is needed to implement any new program. This is perhaps the greatest lesson the book can teach on the topic of successful educational reform of any kind.

These fiscal and administrative difficulties can be particularly oppressive at the community-college level because of the position these institutions occupy in the educational system and their dependence on good will and the funds of local communities. This weakness, however, also contains a strength. At the community-college level, more so than at four-year colleges or universities, the central officers of the institution have the freedom to use their initiative relatively unhampered by the necessities of eliciting consensus. There is less dependence upon support of other members of the constituency. This strength can be a weakness, though, when the central officers are reluctant to embark on new programs.

The involvement and commitment of the president of a college provides the power needed to overcome initial uncertainty and inconvenient setbacks. From the beginning, the program should receive a clean bill of health and generate its own success.

The careful selection of key officers is absolutely critical for the implementation of the international design. They must be able to persist in a diplomatic yet determined manner to overcome the manifold obstacles that present themselves. Faculty resources necessary to establish viable programs can be provided, initially perhaps, only through overtime and some reduction in teaching load.

The timing of the venture is also of paramount importance. This book deals with a decade of almost uninterrupted growth. One wonders how a similar beginning could have been effected if started at a time of decreasing enrollments, shrinking budgets, and a corresponding loss of interest in the world outside the county borders. In the case of one community college, the fortuitous convergence of appropriate timing and good executive leadership permitted the successful fruition of the venture.

In time, supportive staff must be provided and funds for the organization made available. The selection of the Director of International Education should be made, if possible, from the ranks of the faculty. A DIE from the faculty will provide the program with much-needed leverage, which will be absent if a newcomer to the college is asked to organize and launch the international programs.

What has made international activities at the community-college level truly dynamic is the pattern of involving other community colleges (and also upper-division units), first in the immediate area, but ultimately nationwide. The power of one community college to establish overseas programs cannot be compared in effectiveness to the combined thrust of several interested collaborating institutions. The large number of participating students and the rich variety of programs offered through a collective effort are one of the basic ingredients of success.

International ventures at community colleges are susceptible to the "ripple effect." Once a successful academic program is in place overseas, it is much easier for other colleges to adopt similar programs.

International activities in general also possess what might be called welding power. They provide a unifying force by which the vast network of community-college institutions can be knit more closely together.

Thanks to these programs, for the first time the community colleges of the United States have made a joint appearance abroad. Far from remaining obscured by their older and more prominent sister institutions, these colleges have found abroad a network of similar institutions willing and now able to relate to their American counterparts.

The book demonstrates the degree to which the harmonious development of programs overseas is dependent on the home campus and presents a strategy for persuading college administrations to provide solutions to problems that arise in the areas of admission, recording of foreign courses, academic equivalency, grading, financial aid, proper guidance, and counseling. Outside appraisal and evaluation of the effectiveness of these programs is crucial at all stages. Involving administrative officers actively in foreign travel, student guidance, and evaluation generates support and a willingness to solve problems. The commitment of these officers to the aims of international education helps to internationalize the college as a whole. Since the major college officers represent the core power on the campus, their participation is essential.

It is also important to involve the faculty at all stages of the process. Because of the nature of community colleges, the faculty is usually not internationally oriented. Some have never had any academic experience abroad, and most have pursued strictly domestic specializations.

Few are engaged in graduate research that perhaps would expose them to international contacts. Most live in the immediate community and pay close attention to local life and its problems.

To turn such a faculty around is a task that universities seldom have to face. Originating programs abroad within academic departments on campus, with leadership and guidance provided, usually results in immediate involvement, which may quickly become fashionable. In the community college, most initial efforts abroad are short-term and thus provide opportunities for faculty to travel overseas without having to face any problems of absenteeism from regular teaching duties. This type of faculty involvement in turn brings foreign faculty members to the home campus for reciprocating visits. The result is heightened interest at the college and a sense of proprietary involvement by the community-college staff in international activities. Such visits are very important indeed in adding color and stature to the quality of campus life. Once exposed to education abroad, faculty members are more prone to come into contact with or even join professional organizations overseas, as a means of both internationalizing the curriculum and comporting themselves as citizens of the world.

The beneficiaries of all the activities undertaken are, of course, the students. Their lives are touched by these programs in a significant manner. The exposure takes place along two major lines—on and off campus. On campus ideally they encounter programs with much more foreign content and are involved in the excitement of international events and activities. Off campus they benefit, of course, from living and studying abroad, bringing back lasting impressions that influence not only their academic studies but their personalities as well.

The growing presence of foreign students on campus adds international flavor and opportunities for transcultural communication. Students who have studied abroad are more apt to include foreign languages in their academic program upon their return. Some students change majors, while others continue their studies in greater depth for many years.

Some community colleges, after successful experimentation with overseas academic activities, have started to provide special adult-education programs abroad. Though not uniformly successful, enough has been accomplished to extend the reach of these colleges beyond young students to their families. In some cases a new student population has been created, making the college truly a "community" rather than a "junior" college. There is vast potential for the community college as cultural center of its county, and the international dimension can help to realize that potential.

Community colleges, because of constraints of time, subject matter, and student population, generally cannot utilize most existing academic institutions abroad in the development of overseas programs. Hence, a special pattern had to be developed, involving either the creation of specialized programs or linkage with similar institutions or special-purpose colleges overseas. New patterns of study and new modes of operation had to be generated abroad to avoid being locked into a monastic concept.

Organizational innovations abroad fed into a bureaucratic framework established at home, and, as often happens, these new models of operation were quickly accepted, modified to suit local conditions, and finally adopted by other community colleges.

The account of this successful effort would not be complete without placing on record the accumulated tensions and difficulties that had to arise in the development of programs cross-cultural in content, innovative in character, and new to the educational institutions into which they were placed. Specifically, three types of problems can be identified:

1. administrative shortcomings;
2. program failures; and
3. individual problems.

In category one, administrative shortcomings, the following issues deserve particular attention:

First, in spite of the positive rhetoric quoted throughout most of the book, administrative support for international education at most community colleges never reaches or equals the actual support extended to four-year colleges and universities. The old notion that juniors and seniors are somehow more deserving to be exposed to international realities than freshmen and sophomores dies hard. Community colleges looking for support for international programs will perhaps always have to fight an uphill battle. Leadership in the field of international education will continue to rest largely in the hands of four-year colleges and universities in the foreseeable future, and community colleges, often woefully underfunded, will remain in the background. Proportional respresentation, although difficult, is not impossible to reach.

Second, at most community colleges, international education will remain the Cinderella on the scale of values and concerns. Whenever the interests of other programs come into conflict with those of international programs, the inevitable tendency will remain to give the former higher valuation. This will continue to put the international rationale on the defensive, and the administrative ability to deal with such conflicts has to pass a test of tolerance. Somehow ways have to be found to adjust the international objectives to accommodate other purposes which, in turn, will require special ingenuity and make the final accomplishments less than what they could have been. Americans should be conditioned to recognize that an interest in the world is in their own best interest and should take priority over local concerns.

Third, administrative problems continue, owing to unfamiliarity of foreign institutions with the requirements and practices of American community colleges. Examinations have to be scheduled at appropriate times, for which foreign institutions are often not prepared. The relatively easy give and take of American institutions—the discussion method of classroom procedure—is in sharp contrast to the more formal European manner of lecture and presentation and has to fight for acceptance. In many countries there is no tuition payment, and the problem of facilitating the flow of American checks to meet payment deadlines is frequently incomprehensible to educational institutions abroad.

All of these administrative impediments lead to frustrations, special expenditure, effort, and delays. Some are no doubt inevitable in any kind of cooperative venture, while others are due especially to the low priority of international studies in the academic spectrum.

Inevitably, some programs will fail. Out of the multitude of projects, there are always some which, even though well designed, simply do not materialize. These program failures can be placed in two categories.

First, the design and execution go well, but the program fails nonetheless, owing to unforeseen events. All the positive ingredients may be present: administrative backing, experts ready and working, supportive officials, and the need for the program dire and self-evident. Then at a critical point promised financial support does not materialize and the program collapses because no replacement funding can be found in time.

Second, exactly the same conditions exist, except that failure comes from sources that cannot be accounted for. It is only possible to speculate about reasons for the collapse: perhaps the academic preparation of students was not sufficient; participants were not well enough informed about requirements; expenses exceeded expectations; there was too little demand for the program. Any one or a combination of factors may be responsible for the failure of a truly excellent, academically challenging international program.

Finally, personal problems in overseas ventures are inevitable, and community colleges have to bear their share. These difficulties cover a vast range, from drug usage to arrests abroad, from physical accidents to psychological trauma, from automobile mishaps to suicide attempts over a broken heart. There will be that inevitable student who gets lost in the middle of London, Amsterdam, Tokyo, or Mexico City without a passport. However, none of these problems is more than a minor disturbance in the continued successful academic and cultural adaptation of the majority of American college students enrolled in overseas programs.

Twenty years ago only one out of five students started higher education in a community college. Between 1961 and 1980 the number of students in these institutions increased more than six times from under 750,000 to 4,825,000—with more than half of all freshmen students now enrolled in two-year colleges. Clearly, the main responsibility for lower-division education has shifted significantly to the community colleges. International education has to take its place as an important, if not indispensable, ingredient of that educative responsibility. Skeptics will always remain, but options should be available so that students seeking the beginnings of higher education in community colleges may be provided with the benefits of overseas exposure available in other educational institutions.

The most significant point of this book is that a convergence of three elements is essential in the creation of overseas academic programs on the community-college level. These three elements are a president committed and dedicated to the idea; a faculty interested and willing to become involved; and a campus Director of International Education with imagination and organizational talent to serve as a catalyst.

Developing international programs is an ongoing process. There is a great deal of serendipity in the process, as those involved in the programs become flexible enough to reshape their aims in accordance with changing possibilities. Creating and multiplying the various offerings and the alliances that make them possible frequently result in new and unexpected discoveries. Thus, community colleges, which cater to a very young, very local, and often vocationally oriented student population, can establish a presence in an area not related to their original task and yet extremely relevant to the depth of their intellectual life.

Notes

Bibliography

Index

Notes

CHAPTER 1. HISTORY OF INTERNATIONALISM IN INSTITUTIONS OF HIGHER LEARNING

1. Santosh Kumar Das, *The Educational System of the Ancient Hindus* (Calcutta: Mitra Press, 1933). Several other universities such as South Madurai, Kapatapuram, and Madurai existed before Takshasila, but they did not acquire its reputation.

2. M. Arunachalam, *Education in Ancient Tamilnad* (Mayuram: Gandhi Vidyalayam, 1969).

3. Radha Kumud Mookerji, *Ancient Indian Education,* 4th ed. (Delhi: Motilal Banarsidass, 1969), p. 478.

4. Ibid.

5. P. L. Rawat, *History of Indian Education,* 3rd ed. (Agra: Ram Prasad, 1963), p. 98.

6. Mookerji, *Ancient Indian Education,* p. 478.

7. Ibid.

8. Quoted in Das, *Ancient Hindus,* p. 369.

9. Mookerji, *Ancient Indian Education,* p. 564.

10. Ibid.

11. Ibid.

12. J. Rody Kidd, "The First Universities: Takshasila and Nalanda," *Convergence,* 2(3) (1969), 80–83. For a further account of Indian higher education centers see S. P. Chaube, *A His-*

tory of Education in India (Allahabad: Ram Narain Lal Beni Madho, 1965), Chapters VII, X, and XI.

13. Edward D. Myers, *Education in the Perspective of History* (New York: Harper & Bros., 1960), pp. 37–39.

14. Howard S. Galt, *A History of Chinese Educational Institutions,* Vol. 1, *To the End of the Five Dynasties (A.D. 960),* (London: Arthur Probsthain, 1951).

15. Ibid., p. 211, and pp. 367–368. See also Myers, *Education in Perspective,* p. 45.

16. Ping-Ti Ho, *The Ladder of Success in Imperial China* (New York: Columbia University Press, 1962), p. 168.

17. Chang-Tu Hu, ed., *Chinese Education Under Communism* (New York: Teachers College Press, 1974), p. 15.

18. Galt, *Chinese Education;* also, Das, *Ancient Hindus,* pp. 163ff. and 360ff.

19. Hugh L. Keenleyside and A. F. Thomas, *History of Japanese Education and Present Educational Systems* (Tokyo: Hokuseido Press, 1937), p. 34. See also George Z. F. Bereday and Shigea Masui, *American Education Through Japanese Eyes* (Honolulu: University of Hawaii Press, 1973), Appendix 3, p. 248.

20. George B. Sansom, *Japan: A Short Cultural History,* rev. ed. (New York: Appleton-Century-Crofts, 1962), p. 89. See also George B. Sansom, *A History of Japan to 1334* (Stanford: Stanford University Press, 1958).

21. C. Elgood, "Persian Science," in A. J. Arberry, ed., *The Legacy of Persia* (Oxford: Clarendon Press, 1953), pp. 310–311.

22. Richard N. Frye, *The Heritage of Persia* (Cleveland: The World Publishing Co., 1963), p. 221.

23. Ibid.

24. Ibid.

25. Mehdi Kakosteen, *History of Islamic Origins of Western Education A.D. 800–1350, with an Introduction to Medieval Muslim Education* (Boulder: University of Colorado Press, 1964), pp. 20ff.

26. Harrison G. Gough and William A. McCormack, *An Exploratory Evaluation of Education Abroad* (Berkeley: University of California Press, 1967), p. 6.

27. Ibid., p. 6.

28. Bayard Dodge, *Al-Azhar: A Milennium of Muslim Learning* (Washington, D.C.: Middle East Institute, 1961), p. 45.

29. Frederick A. G. Beck, *Greek Education 450–350 B.C.* (New

York: Barnes & Noble, 1964), p. 161; and Paul Monroe, *Source Book of the History of Education for the Greek and Roman Periods* (London: MacMillan & Co., 1939), p. 62.

30. James L. Jarrett, *The Educational Theories of the Sophists* (New York: Teachers College Press, 1969), p. 18.

31. Ibid., pp. 26–27.

32. Plato, "Protagoras," in *The Portable Plato* (New York: The Viking Press, 1948), p. 54.

33. See John W. H. Walden, *The Universities of Ancient Greece* (New York: Charles Scribner's Sons, 1909), pp. 15–19. See also Martin L. Clarke, *Higher Education in the Ancient World* (Albuquerque: University of New Mexico Press, 1971).

34. W. W. Capes, *University Life in Ancient Athens* (New York: G. E. Stechert Company, 1922), pp. 2–3 (originally published, 1877). Pericles viewed Athens as both "open to the world" (p. 96) and as "an education to the Greeks" (pp. 125–126). See C. M. Bowra, *Periclean Athens* (New York: Dial Press, 1971) for an understanding of the interplay between imperialism, the philosophy of empire, the intellectual revolution, and the effects of the various wars upon Athens.

35. Clarke, *Higher Education in the Ancient World,* p. 59.

36. Ibid., p. 71.

37. Capes, *University Life in Ancient Athens,* p. 97.

38. Ibid., p. 98.

39. Ibid., p. 102.

40. Walden, *The Universities of Ancient Greece,* p. 52.

41. R. Freeman Butts, *The Education of the West. A Formative Chapter in the History of Civilization* (New York: McGraw-Hill, 1973), p. 111. See also James Bowen, *A History of Western Education,* Vol. 1, *The Ancient World: Orient and Mediterranean, 2000 B.C.–A.D. 1054* (London: Methuen, 1972).

42. Paul Monroe, *A Brief Course in the History of Education* (New York: Macmillan, 1924), p. 94.

43. Guy Metraux, "Cross-Cultural Education Through the Ages," *International Social Science Bulletin,* 8(4) (1956), 577–586, sees the educational travel of the young Romans to Greece in order to acquire knowledge as the exemplification of the primary function of such travel. The Roman historian Tacitus used his travels to Greece and other countries as reference points for his comparative education reports on the Germans and other peoples.

44. H. I. Marrou, *A History of Education in Antiquity* (New York: Mentor Books, 1964), pp. 255–256.

45. Butts, *Education of the West,* pp. 123ff.

46. Stanley F. Bonner, *Education in Ancient Rome: From the Elder Cato to the Younger Pliny* (Berkeley: University of California Press, 1977), p. 90.

47. Ibid.

48. Marrou, *History of Education in Antiquity,* pp. 296–297.

49. Ibid., p. 297.

50. Ibid., pp. 297–298.

51. Ibid., p. 298.

52. Some scholars, such as Seneca, were not born within the boundaries of Rome but were accepted as full-fledged Romans because of their cultural achievements.

53. Stephen d'Irsay, *Histoire des universités françaises et étrangères des origines à nos jours,* Vol. 1, *Moyen Age et Renaissance* (Paris: A. Picard, 1933–1935), p. 146.

54. Erich Ashby and Mary Anderson, *Universities: British, Indian, African* (Cambridge: Harvard University Press, 1966), p. 4. See also Gabriel Compayre, *Abelard and the Origin and Early History of Universities* (New York: Charles Scribner's Sons, 1893), p. 69. He notes that "learned peregrinations were then obligatory for all students." However, not all cities appreciated the mobility of their students. Florence, for example, attempted to impose fines upon those who studied outside the city.

55. Pearl Kibre, *Scholarly Privileges in the Middle Ages* (Cambridge, Mass.: Medieval Academy of America, 1962).

56. "The University of Paris with its four nations, the common mother of all northern universities, the recognized fountainhead of the streams of knowledge which watered the whole Christian world, could claim something of that international character which medieval theory accorded to the papacy and the empire." Hastings Rashdall, *The Universities of Europe in the Middle Ages,* Vol. 1, eds. F. M. Powicke and A. B. Emden (London: Oxford University Press, 1936), p. 573. See also Gordon Lett, *Paris and Oxford Universities in the Thirteenth and Fourteenth Centuries: An Institutional and Intellectual History* (New York: John Wiley, 1968).

57. Helene Wierusowski, *The Medieval University: Masters, Students, Learning* (Princeton, N.J.: D. Van Nostrand, 1966), p. 22.

58. Ibid. See also Peter Abelard, *The Story of My Misfortunes,* trans. Henry Adams Bellows (New York: Macmillan, 1922), pp. v, 3, 4, 9–11.

59. Ibid., p. 21.

60. Ibid.

61. Gough and McCormack, *Education Abroad,* p. 6.

62. Pearl Kibre, *The Nations in the Medieval Universities* (Cambridge, Mass.: Medieval Academy of America, 1948), p. 13.

63. Gray Cowan Boyce, *The English-German Nation in the University of Paris During the Middle Ages* (Burges: St. Catherine Press, 1927), p. 28. See also Astrik L. Gabriel, *Garlandia, Studies in the History of the Medieval University* (Frankfurt am Main: Josef Knecht, 1969), pp. 169–170.

64. Gough and McCormack, *Education Abroad,* p. 6.

65. Felix H. Hirsch, "The Migration of Scholars in History," *School and Society* 45 (19 June 1937), 833.

66. Ibid.

67. Ibid., p. 834.

68. Kibre, *The Nations in the Medieval Universities,* p. 109.

69. Rashdall, *The Universities of Europe in the Middle Ages,* Vol. 1, p. 581, and d'Irsay, *Histoire des universités françaises,* p. 207.

70. *The World of Learning 1974–75,* 25th ed. (London: Europa Publications, 1974), Vols. 1 and 2.

71. R. H. Samuel and R. Hinton Thomas, *Education and Society in Modern Germany* (London: Routledge & Kegan Paul, 1949), p. 114.

72. Frank Pierrepont Graves, *A History of Education During the Middle Ages and the Transition to Modern Times* (New York: Macmillan, 1914), pp. 149–150.

73. H. G. Good, *A History of Western Education* (New York: Macmillan, 1960), p. 106. See also Rashdall, *The Universities of Europe in the Middle Ages,* Vol. 3, p. 352.

74. Butts, *Education of the West,* p. 197. See also William W. Brickman, "Some Review Data on History of Education," *Comparative Education Review,* 8(3) (December 1964); and Nicholas Hans, "The Historical Evolution of Internationalism," in George Z. F. Bereday and J. A. Lauwerys, eds., *The Yearbook of Education—1964: Education and International Life* (New York: Harcourt, Brace & World, 1964), pp. 21–32.

75. Reinhold Schairer, *Die Studenten im Internationalen Kulturleben* (Münster i. W.: Aschendorffsche Verlagsbuchhandlung, 1927), p. 9.

76. T. H. Huxley's interest extended beyond the sciences "as he proved by joining in 1865 the recently formed International Education Society. . . . The Society, one of whose objects was to help the cause of European peace, set up at Isleworth the International College to give a liberal education in preparation for commerce and the professions." John W. Adamson, *English Education: 1789–1902* (Cambridge: University Press, 1930), p. 393.

77. T. H. Huxley, "A Liberal Education and Where to Find It," in Frederick Eby and Charles Flinn Arrowood, eds., *The Development of Modern Education in Theory, Organization and Practice* (New York: Prentice-Hall, 1940), p. 731.

78. Ibid.

79. Quoted in William W. Brickman, "International Relations in Higher Education," in William W. Brickman and Sidney Lehrer, eds., *A Century of Higher Education* (Westport, Conn.: Greenwood Press, 1962), p. 212.

80. George Altomare, "The United Nations University: Origins, Founding and Future" (unpublished doctoral dissertation, Teachers College, Columbia University, 1977). Segments of the appendix to the dissertation (unused in the original manuscript) were made available by the author during the preparation of the foregoing summary. His generosity is gratefully acknowledged.

CHAPTER 2. COMMUNITY COLLEGES AND
OVERSEAS ACADEMIC PROGRAMS

1. The earliest American programs organized for study abroad were initiated by women's colleges in the East. Marymount and Delaware established the first programs in Paris in 1923, followed by Smith in Paris and Rosary College in Fribourg two years later. See Harrison G. Gough and William A. McCormack, *An Exploratory Evaluation of Education Abroad* (Berkeley: University of California Press, 1967), p. 9.

2. See President's Commission on Foreign Language and International Studies, *Report: Background Papers and Studies* (Wash-

ington, D.C.: U.S. Government Printing Office, 1979). See also *Strength Through Wisdom: A Critique of U.S. Capabilities* (Washington, D.C.: U.S. Government Printing Office, 1979).

3. *Rockland Community College Bulletin,* 1972/73, p. 1.

4. Ibid.

5. President's Commission, *Report: Strength Through Wisdom.*

6. George Z. F. Bereday, *Universities for All: International Perspectives on Mass Higher Education* (San Francisco: Jossey-Bass, 1973), p. 58.

7. James W. Thornton, Jr., *The Community Junior College* (New York: John Wiley & Sons, 1972), p. 299.

8. Ibid.

9. Bereday, *Universities for All,* p. 67. See also Leland L. Medsker, *The Junior College: Progress and Prospect* (New York: McGraw-Hill, 1960), pp. 174–175.

10. Bereday, *Universities for All,* p. 58.

11. State University of New York (SUNY), Central Administration, Office of International Programs, Department of International Education, "Goal Statement" (draft), Albany, N.Y., August 1972, rev. March 1975.

12. State University of New York (SUNY), Central Administration, Office of International Programs, Department of International Education, "Statement on Overseas Academic Programs" (draft), Albany, N.Y., 1976.

13. Ibid.

14. State University of New York (SUNY), International Studies and World Affairs Committee, "Position Paper," presented at a Conference on International Education, Syracuse, N.Y., March 25–26, 1976.

15. Ibid.

16. Ibid.

CHAPTER 3. THE ROCKLAND MODEL

1. *Rockland Community College Catalog,* 1969/70, p. 7.

2. Originally 26 acres, now enlarged to 175 acres.

3. Not to be confused with the State University of New York or New York University, the largest private university in the country, located in New York City. The following description of

the University of the State of New York is given in State of New York, *Legislative Manual* (1975), p. 655:

"The Regents of The University of the State of New York were established and incorporated by act of the Legislature in 1784. Their continuance is provided for by the Constitution of the State. There are 15 Regents—four more than the existing judicial districts in the State—who are elected, one each year, by the Legislature.

"The University of the State of New York, which the Regents govern, is the most comprehensive educational organization in the world. It includes in its constituent membership and has under its supervision all public schools of the State, and also, in the terms of the law, includes, all institutions which are now or may hereafter be incorporated by this State, and such libraries, museums, institutions, schools, organizations and agencies for education as may be admitted to or incorporated by The University.

"Among their specific powers, the Regents are authorized to exercise legislative functions concerning the educational system of the State; to determine its educational policies, and make rules for corporate educational institutions and organizations; they may confer degrees; they have power to visit and inspect educational institutions of the State; they register domestic and foreign educational institutions and fix the values of degrees, diplomas and certificates from all parts of the world; and they supervise the preliminary education requirements for admission to the practice of law, medicine, dentistry, veterinary medicine, pharmacy, optometry, podiatry, massage, engineering and land surveying, architecture, ophthalmic dispensing, psychology and to practice as a registered or practical nurse, a certified public accountant, certified shorthand reporter, and a chiropractor. The chief officers of The University are the Chancellor and the President of The University, who is also the Commissioner of Education.

"The Commissioner of Education is the chief executive officer of the Regents and of the state educational system. He is appointed by the Regents and serves at their pleasure."

4. *Rockland Community College Bulletin,* 1972/73.

5. *Catalog,* p. 3.

6. Ibid.

7. "Article 126: Community Colleges and State-Aided Four-Year Colleges," in *McKinney's Consolidated Laws of New York Annotated* (St. Paul: West Publishing Co., 1972), pp. 128–151.

8. *Bulletin,* p. 3.

9. Ibid.

10. As of July 1, 1975, the eight community colleges sponsored by the New York City Board of Higher Education ceased to be under the program of the State University of New York and became part of the City University of New York.

11. SUNY's efforts to internationalize the University came at a time of rapid growth. The total student population grew from 226,022 in 1967 to 409,611 in 1974 and the community college population from 115,550 to 220,161 in the same period.

12. Dr. Glenn Olds was installed as the first dean of the Center and functioned in that capacity until he left SUNY to join the staff for the election of Richard Nixon to his first presidency. He later became successively special assistant for policy and manpower development to the president, a United States ambassador, a representative to the United Nations Economic and Social Council, and president of Kent State University. See Jacques Press Cattell, ed., *Leaders in Education,* 5th ed. (New York and London: R. R. Bowker, 1974), p. 819. Dr. Ivan J. Putman, a distinguished international educator, became university dean at ISWA in 1968 and subsequently director of the SUNY Central Office of International Programs from 1973 to 1977.

13. Albany, Binghamton, Buffalo, Stony Brook.

14. Such as financing, logistics, timing (re: academic calendar), admission, transfer of credits, etc.

15. Service learning is an attempt to fuse two powerful approaches to learning: learning through experience and learning from a teacher. In service learning, the teacher is a mentor who helps each student design a learning program whose core is the experience of community service.

While the majority of students enrolled in the ICC Israel Program continue to study conventionally organized curricula in a formal classroom of traditional host colleges and universities, this project is designed as an alternative for those students who wish to combine classroom instruction with the opportunity to serve and work.

16. A learning contract is an agreement between a mentor, representing the institution, and a student. The student, guided by the mentor, identifies the specific "learning objectives" for that contract and specifies the "learning activities" through which these

objectives are to be obtained. Learning activities may include individual and group seminars and tutorials, practical community experience (fieldwork), assigned readings, and formal classes. The learning contract clearly spells out the evaluation procedures to be followed: usually a combination of papers, examinations, projects, tapes, etc. The evaluation methods, as all contract components, are agreed upon in advance and can be altered or modified only by mutual agreement of the mentor and student. When the terms of the contract are fulfilled, the mentor, in concert with the tutors and/or fieldwork supervisors, assigns a grade and authorizes the awarding of the agreed-upon credits.

CHAPTER 4. INTERINSTITUTIONAL, STATE, AND NATIONAL COOPERATION

1. For example: J. H. Pestalozzi's (1746–1827) school at Yverdon received great acclaim and national recognition as well as support. Yet, upon his retirement from the school and even prior to his death Yverdon ceased to exist. More recently, A. S. Neill's (1883–1973) Summerhill School at Leiston gained virtually worldwide attention in the educational field and, again, the institution died with its founder.

2. Later renamed SUNY Advisory Committee on International Programs.

3. Letter from the Ecumenical Council of New York to Seymour Eskow, President of Rockland Community College, March 23, 1972.

4. Edmund J. Gleazer, Jr. (President, American Association of Community and Junior Colleges), "Memorandum to Community College Presidents," March 24, 1975.

5. Ibid.

6. American Association of Community and Junior Colleges, *International/Intercultural Consortium Brochure,* issued at the 56th conference of the AACJC, 1976 (available from AACJC, One Dupont Circle, Washington, D.C. 20036). The I/IC was officially established in 1976.

7. Edmund J. Gleazer, Jr., "Statement of the Office of International Programs of the AACJC," paper presented at Workshop

on Intercultural Studies Program Development, Washington, D.C., 1975.

8. The first community college was established in 1892.

9. Gleazer, "Statement of the Office of International Programs of the AACJC."

10. Ibid.

11. Ibid.

12. Ibid.

13. Edmund J. Gleazer, Jr., "Editorial," *Community and Junior College Journal* 46(7) (April 1976), 5.

14. Ibid.

15. AACJC, *Brochure.*

CHAPTER 5. THE COLLEGE CONSORTIUM
FOR INTERNATIONAL STUDIES

1. College Consortium for International Studies, *Agreement,* revised June 12, 1981, Preamble, p. 1.

2. Ibid.

3. Ibid., "Purposes of the Consortium," No. 2.

4. Ibid., No. 4.

5. Ibid., "Organization of the Consortium," p. 2.

6. Ibid.

7. College Consortium for International Studies, *Bylaws,* revised June 12, 1981, Article 1, p. 1.

8. CCIS, *Agreement.*

9. Ibid.

10. Ibid.

11. CCIS, *Bylaws,* Article 3, p. 2.

12. Ibid., Article 2, No. 5, p. 2.

13. College Consortium for International Studies, *Study Abroad Program Policies,* revised June 12, 1981, No. 7, p. 1.

14. Ibid., No. 16, p. 2.

15. College Consortium for International Studies, *General Information,* revised June 12, 1981, Service Learning, p. 2.

16. Ibid.

17. Ibid., Contract/Independent Study, p. 2.

18. Ibid.

CHAPTER 7. IMPACT OF INTERNATIONAL
PROGRAMS ON FACULTY AND STUDENTS

1. A foreign student is defined as any "individual who must prove to a U.S. consular official that he wishes to enter the U.S. temporarily and solely for the purposes of study and that he has a permanent residence in a foreign country which he has no intention of abandoning, Act 101(a)(15)(F)." See *Adviser's Manual of Federal Regulations Affecting Foreign Students and Scholars,* issued by National Association for Foreign Student Affairs, 1860 19th Street, N.W., Washington, D.C. 20009.

Bibliography

Abelard, Peter. *The Story of My Misfortunes,* trans. Henry Adams Bellows. New York: Macmillan, 1922.

Ablin, F. "Decision-Making in Soviet Higher Education: A Documentary History." *Soviet Education,* 12 (July 1970), 3–287.

Ackerman, W. C. "Private Support Activities in International Education." *International Educational and Cultural Exchange,* 6 (Fall 1970), 1–13.

Adams, F. "State Colleges Go Global; International Study Centers." *International Educational and Cultural Exchange,* 8 (Summer 1972), 65–68.

Adams, V. A. "Hostos Community College Mixes Dreams and Reality." *College Management,* 7 (March 1972), 5–11.

Adamson, J. M. "Fulbright to India." *International Educational and Cultural Exchange,* 6 (Summer 1970), 9–26.

Adamson, John W. *English Education: 1789–1902.* Cambridge: University Press, 1930.

Adiseshiah, M. S. "Tasks for the International Education Year." *School and Society,* 98 (Summer 1970), 296–298.

Alger, C. F. "International Organizations and World Order: Social Science as a Source of New Perspectives." *National*

Council for the Social Studies Yearbook, 38 (1968), 54–77.

Altbach, G. *Higher Education in Developing Countries, A Selected Bibliography.* Cambridge: Harvard University International Affairs, 1970.

Altomare, George. "The United Nations University: Origins, Founding and Future." Unpublished Doctoral Dissertation, Teachers College, Columbia University, 1977.

American Association of Community and Junior Colleges. *International/Intercultural Consortium Brochure,* issued at the 56th conference of the AACJC, 1976. Available from AACJC, One Dupont Circle, Washington, D.C. 20036.

Apetz, W., et al. *New Jersey Community Colleges—The First Ten Years, 1963–1973; A Report of the New Jersey Council of Community Colleges to the State Legislature.* Trenton: New Jersey State Department of Higher Education, Office of Community College Programs, 1973. (ERIC Document Reproduction Service No. ED 105 945.)

Arberry, A. J., ed. *The Legacy of Persia.* Oxford: Clarendon Press, 1953.

Armistead, E. *The Virginia Community College System: An Examination After Its First Decade.* Tallahassee: Florida State and Regional Higher Education Center, 1977. (ERIC Document Reproduction Service No. ED 143 411.)

Arunachalam, M. *Education in Ancient Tamiland.* Mayuram: Gandhi Vidyalayam, 1969.

Ashby, Erich, and Anderson, Mary. *Universities: British, Indian, African.* Cambridge: Harvard University Press, 1966.

Bailey, S. K., ed. "Higher Education in the World Community." *Lexington,* American Council on Education pub., 1977.

Banks, Y. A. "Cultural Pluralism and the Schools." *Educational Digest,* 40 (April 1975), 21–23.

Barker, H. K. "International Education and the Professional Associations." *Phi Delta Kappan,* 51 (January 1970), 244–246.

Barrutia, R. "Study Abroad." *Modern Language Journal,* 55 (April 1971), 232–234.

Bass, B. M. "American Advisor Board." *Journal of Applied Behavioral Science,* 7 (May 1971), 285–308.

Baughman, M. D. "Global Education." *Contemporary Education,* 42 (November 1970), 80–84.

Beals, L. "Experiment in International Education." *Junior College Journal,* 40 (April 1970), 35–37.

Beals, R. L., and Humphrey, N. D. *No Question to Learning.* Minneapolis: University of Minnesota Press, 1957.

Beck, Frederick A. G. *Greek Education 450–350 B.C.* New York: Barnes & Noble, 1964.

Becker, J. M. "International and Cross-Cultural Experiences." *Association for Supervision and Curriculum Development Yearbook* (1973), 103–124.

Benedict, R. C. "SUNY-Thorz Academic Exchange." *International Educational and Cultural Exchange,* 13 (Summer 1977), 34–39.

Berckx, P. H. "Organization of a European Information System for the Purposes of Recognizing Studies Pursued Abroad." *Western European Education,* 6 (Fall 1974), 5–59.

Bereday, George Z. F. *Universities for All: International Perspectives on Mass Higher Education.* San Francisco: Jossey-Bass, 1973.

———, and Masui, Shigea. *American Education Through Japanese Eyes.* Honolulu: University of Hawaii Press, 1973.

———, and Pennar, J., eds. *The Politics of Soviet Education.* New York: Frederick A. Praeger, 1960.

Bernier, N., ed. "Multicultural Education: Its Effective Management; Symposium." *The American Association of Colleges for Teacher Education Yearbook* (1974), 77–90.

Bethke, B. E. "Learning to Teach More Than English." *International Educational and Cultural Exchange,* 12 (Spring 1977), 31–35.

Beynon, R. "Curriculum, the Teacher, the Years Ahead." *Education,* 90 (Spring 1969), 72–75.

Bidwell, P. W. *Undergraduate Education in Foreign Affairs.* New York: King's Crown Press, 1962.

Billigmeier, R. H., and Forman, D. C. "Göttingen in Retrospect. A Longitudinal Assessment of the University of California's Education Abroad Program in Göttingen by 1965–66 Participants." *International Review of Education,* 21(2) (1975), 217–230.

Bloom, J. M. "Without a Vocabulary: A Story of a Disadvantaged Teacher." *Physical Education,* 27 (May 1970), 71–72.

Bodner, G. "Bridging the Culture Gap." *New York State Education,* 58 (April 1971), 27–28.

Bonner, Stanley F. *Education in Ancient Rome: From the Elder Cato to the Younger Pliny.* Berkeley: University of California Press, 1977.

Bowen, James. *A History of Western Education,* Vol. 1, *The Ancient World: Orient and Mediterranean, 2000 B.C.–A.D. 1054.* London: Methuen, 1972.

Bowra, C. M. *Periclean Athens.* New York: Dial Press, 1971.

Boyce, Gray Cowan. *The English-German Nation in the University of Paris During the Middle Ages.* Burges: St. Catherine Press, 1927.

Brann, E. T. H. "Conditions of Exchange." *International Educational and Cultural Exchange,* 12 (Spring 1977), 3–9.

Brembeck, C. S. "American University Response to Problems of Development Overseas." *Viewpoints,* 47 (September 1971), 101–129.

Brickman, William W. "Delusion of Cultural Detente. World Congress of Peace Forces." *Intellect,* 102 (Summer 1974), 480–481.

————. "International Element in Teacher Education." *School and Society,* 97 (December 1969), 474–475.

————. "International Relations in Higher Education." In William W. Brickman and Sidney Lehrer, eds., *A Century of Higher Education.* Westport, Conn.: Greenwood Press, 1962.

————. "Some Review Data on History of Education." *Comparative Education Review,* 8(3) (December 1964), 281–284.

————, and Lehrer, Sidney, eds. *A Century of Higher Education.* Westport, Conn.: Greenwood Press, 1962.

Brunner, K. A. "Historical Development of the Junior College Philosophy." *Junior College Journal,* 40 (April 1970), 30–34.

Bryan, M., and Pavord, W. "Lost and Not Yet Found: International Commitment for Universities." *Intellect,* 101 (March 1973), 377–380.

Burn, B. B. "Changes and Exchanges in Higher Education: U.S.A. and Germany." *International Educational and Cultural Exchange,* 8 (Winter 1972–73), 63–68.

Bushnell, D. S. *Organizing for Change: New Priorities for Community Colleges.* New York: McGraw-Hill, 1973.

Butt, M. "Role and Rationale of Educational Aid in Developing Countries: An Impending Crisis of Confidence." *Viewpoints,* 47 (September 1971), 191–203.

Butts, R. Freeman. *The Education of the West: A Formative Chapter in the History of Civilization.* New York: McGraw-Hill, 1973.

Caldwell, O. J. "Need for Intercultural Education in Our Universities." *Phi Delta Kappan,* 52 (May 1971), 544–545.

Campos, C. "Students and Europe." *University Quarterly,* 26 (Summer 1972), 280–309.

Capes, W. W. *University Life in Ancient Athens.* New York: G. E. Stechert Company, 1922.

Carr, W. G. "Teachers and International Education." *American Association of Colleges for Teacher Education Yearbook,* 22 (1969), 73–78.

Cattell, Jacques Press, ed. *Leaders in Education,* 5th ed. New York and London: R. R. Bowker, 1974.

Cervi, M., and Manfred, S. "Physical Education: A Semester in Germany." *Journal of Health, Physical Education, Recreation,* 45 (February 1974), 93–94.

Chabe, A. M. "Soviet Education: Its Implications for United States Education." *Educational Forum,* 41 (November 1976), 15–19.

Chabert, M. "Why Take a Foreign Civilization Course?"

Modern Language Journal, 60 (September 1976), 248–
    251.
Chadwick, C., and Morgan, R. M. "Educational Technology
    Assistance for Developing Countries." *Educational Tech-
    nology,* 11 (September 1971), 49–53.
Chambers, M. M. *Above High School.* Danville, Ill.: Inter-
    state Printers and Publishers, 1970.
Chaube, S. P. *A History of Education in India.* Allahabad:
    Ram Narain Lal Beni Madho, 1965.
Chen, T. "International Aspects of Education in Communist
    China." *Phi Delta Kappan,* 51 (January 1970), 251–255.
Cheng, S. C., and Edwards, R. "Individual Versus Coopera-
    tive Research in Comparative Education: An Extension of
    the I.E.A. Enquiry to Hong Kong." *Comparative Educa-
    tion,* 7 (December 1971), 107–119.
Christensen, L., et al. "Evaluating Non-Sponsored Study
    Abroad." *College and University,* 48 (Summer 1973), 650–
    655.
Clarke, Martin L. *Higher Education in the Ancient World.*
    Albuquerque: University of New Mexico Press, 1971.
Cohen, H. M. *Dateline '79. Heretical Concepts for the Com-
    munity College.* Beverly Hills, Cal.: Glencoe Press, 1969.
Coleman, J. S. *Education and Political Development.* Prince-
    ton, N.J.: Princeton University Press, 1965.
College Consortium for International Studies. *Agreement,*
    revised June 12, 1981.
————. *Bylaws,* revised June 12, 1981.
————. *General Information,* revised June 12, 1981.
————. *Study Abroad Program Policies,* revised June 12,
    1981.
Commager, H. S. "Education and International Community."
    Phi Delta Kappan, 15 (January 1970), 280–284.
Commandy, H. S. "Creative Alternatives in International
    Education." *International Educational and Cultural Ex-
    change,* 11 (Winter 1976), 5–9.
Compayre, Gabriel. *Abelard and the Origin and Early History
    of Universities.* New York: Charles Scribner's Sons, 1893.

Conger, G. R., and Schultz, R. C. "Leonard V. Koos: Patriarch of the Junior College." *Junior College Journal,* 40 (March 1970), 26–31.

Coombs, P. H. *New Paths to Learning.* New York: The International Council for Educational Development, 1973.

Cormack, M. L. "International Educational Exchange: Visas to What?" *International Educational and Cultural Exchange,* 5 (Fall 1969), 46–64.

———. "Revolution and Relevance: International Educational Exchange." *The Record,* 71 (December 1969), 265–275.

Corrie, B. A. "Monument to Greco-American Relations Through Sports. Gymnasium-Auditorium at Anatolia (Salonika) College." *Journal of Physical Education and Recreation,* 48 (November/December, 1977), 65–66.

Cosper, C. "Human Rights and International Education." *School and Society* (November 1969), 457–458.

Court, D. "Experience of Higher Education in East Africa: The University of Dar Es Salaam as a New Model?" (Tanzania). *Comparative Education,* 11 (October 1975), 193–218.

Das, Santosh Kumar. *The Educational System of the Ancient Hindus.* Calcutta: Mitra Press, 1933.

Dean of Students' Office, Rockland Community College. Personal Interview, Dr. J. Lambert, March 16, 1976.

Dinkmeyer, E., et al. "Study Abroad in Asia." *College and University,* 48 (Summer 1973), 655–669.

d'Irsay, Stephen. *Histoire des universités françaises et étrangères des origines à nos jours,* Vol. 1, *Moyen Age et Renaissance.* Paris: A. Picard, 1933–1935.

Dodge, Bayard. *Al-Azhar: A Millennium of Muslim Learning.* Washington, D.C.: Middle East Institute, 1961.

Donn, P. A., and Hollis, J. W. "Counselor Education Abroad: Selected Programs." *Counselor Education and Supervision,* 12 (December 1972), 137–143.

Drapela, V. S. "Comparative Guidance Through International

Study." *Personnel and Guidance Journal,* 53 (February 1975), 438–445.

Du Bois, E. E. "Demise of the Church-Related College: A Case Study." *Journal of Education,* 153 (December 1970), 5–15.

Dyerson, D., et al. "Non-Sponsored Study Abroad, Any Credit?" *College and University,* 44 (Summer 1969), 515–517.

Eby, Frederick, and Arrowood, Charles Flinn, eds. *The Development of Modern Education: Theory, Organization and Practice.* New York: Prentice-Hall, 1940.

Ecumenical Council of New York. Letter to Seymour Eskow, President of Rockland Community College, March 23, 1972.

Eide, I., ed. *Students as Links Between Cultures: A Cross-Cultural Survey Based on UNESCO Students.* Oslo: Universitetsfarlenget, 1970.

Ekgol'm, I. K. "International Education: A Means of Ideological Expansion of American Imperialism," trans. M. Vale. *Soviet Education,* 11 (August 1969), 31–44.

Elam, S. M. "Goals of (and Obstacles to) First International Education Year 1970." *Phi Delta Kappan,* 51 (January 1970), 229.

Elgood, C. "Persian Science." In A. J. Arberry, ed., *The Legacy of Persia.* Oxford: Clarendon Press, 1953.

Elvin, H. L. "International Education Year 1970." *International Review of Education,* 16(4) (1970), 390–392.

England, G. W., and Lee, R. "Relationship Between Managerial Values and Managerial Success in the United States, Japan, India and Australia." *Journal of Applied Psychology,* 59 (August 1974), 411–419.

Fakouri, M. E. "International Education Year." *Contemporary Education,* 42 (November 1970), 60.

Fantini, A. E. "Formula for Success: Camp Plus Young Americans Plus New Language." *International Educational Exchange,* 8 (Fall 1972), 62–69.

Farrar, M. "European School, Uccle, Brussels." *Trends in Education,* 2 (Summer 1977), 30–34.

Feather, N. T., and Raphelson, A. C. "Fear of Success in Australian and American Student Groups: Motive or Sex-Role Stereotype?" *Journal of Personality,* 42 (June 1974), 190–201.

Fernandez, R. M. "Staffing Instructional Materials and Bilingual-Bicultural Education. Materials Acquisition Project, San Diego, California." *California Journal of Educational Research,* 25 (November 1974), 274–280.

Fersh, S. H. "Education in a World of Nations." *Contemporary Education,* 42 (November 1970), 69–73.

Finchum, G. A. "African Experience: Contemporary Pedagogue." *International Educational and Cultural Exchange,* 8 (Fall 1972), 54–61.

Fischer, G. D., and Maheu, R. "Road to Peace and Progress." *Today's Education,* 59 (May 1970), 20–23.

Fisher, R., and Palsey, A. "Exchange Programme, or Program. Great Britain and United States." *The New York Times Educational Supplement,* July 17, 1970, p. 78.

Flack, M. J. "Cultural Diplomacy: Blindspot in International Affairs Textbooks." *International Educational and Cultural Exchange,* 8 (Winter 1972–73), 11–18.

Flynn, J. R. "Price of Power: Universities in America and New Zealand." *University Quarterly,* 27 (Autumn 1973), 383–393.

Forman, B. "Travel Experiences Enrich Teaching." *Instructor,* 81 (January 1972), 97.

Fox, J. H. R. "Educational Technology and Overseas Exchange." *Universities Quarterly,* 24 (Autumn 1970), 453–464.

Frankel, C. *The Neglected Aspect of Foreign Affairs.* Washington, D.C.: The Brookings Institute, 1965.

Frankie, R. J. "Legal Aspects of Authorization and Control in Junior Colleges: A Summary (1936–1970)." *College and University,* 46 (Winter 1971), 148–154.

————, and Du Bois, E. E. "Community-Junior College in Historical and Cultural Perspective." *School and Society,* 99 (January 1971), 45–47.

Fraser, S. E. "China's International, Cultural and Educational Relations: With Selected Bibliography." *Comparative Education Review,* 13 (February 1969), 60–87.

————. "Sino-Soviet Educational Relations: A Recent Episode." *School and Society,* 100 (January 1972), 54–58.

————, ed. *Governmental Policy and International Education.* New York: John Wiley & Sons, 1965.

————, and Brickman, William W. *A History of International and Comparative Education.* New York: Scott, Foresman & Co., 1968.

French, P. L. "January in Kenya: Enriching Field Seminar." *International Educational and Cultural Exchange,* 8 (Spring 1973), 47–52.

Frye, Richard N. *The Heritage of Persia.* Cleveland: The World Publishing Co., 1963.

Fulbright, J. W. "Quarter-Century of Educational Exchange: Values and Future Perspectives." *School and Society,* 100 (Summer 1972), 298–300.

Gabriel, Alstrik L. *Garlandia, Studies in the History of the Medieval University.* Frankfurt am Main: Josef Knecht, 1969.

Gallivan, F. "Health Education: International but National; Health Educators and School Nurses at Department of Defense Dependent Schools." *Health Education,* 8 (September/October 1977), 7–8.

Galt, Howard S. *A History of Chinese Educational Institutions,* Vol. 1, *To the End of the Five Dynasties (A.D. 960).* London: Arthur Probsthain, 1951.

Garcia, P. "Teacher Fulfills Desire for Foreign Travel Plus Humanitarian Service." *Delta Kappa Gamma Bulletin,* 37 (Fall 1970), 18–21.

Garrard, L. G. "Other Side of Teaching: International Opportunities." *Journal of Home Economics,* 37 (April 1974), 37–38.

Garraty, J. A., and Adams, W. *From Main Street to the Left Bank.* Lansing: Michigan State University Press, 1959.

Gaudino, R. L. *The Indian University.* New York: International Publications Service, 1965.

Gayfer, M. "International Council for Adult Education." *Adult Leadership,* 23 (November 1974), 130–132.

Gerber, D. R. "William Watts Folwell and the Idea of the Junior College." *Junior College Journal,* 41 (March 1971), 50–53.

Ginzberg, E. "American Professor at Asian Universities." *International Educational and Cultural Exchanges,* 5 (Summer 1969), 12–19.

Gleazer, Edmund J., Jr. "Editorial." *Community and Junior College Journal,* 46(7) (April 1976).

———. "International Assembly on Junior College Education, Honolulu." *Junior College Journal,* 40 (October 1969), 7.

———. "International Thrust." *Community and Junior College Journal,* 48 (December 1977/January 1978), 2.

———. "Memorandum to Community College Presidents," March 24, 1975. (Typewritten.)

———. "New Mandate for Coordination." *New Directions for Community Colleges,* 2(2) (Summer 1974), 1–8.

———. *Project Focus: A Forecast Study of Community Colleges.* New York: McGraw-Hill, 1973.

———. "Statement of the Office of International Programs of the AACJC." Paper presented at Workshop on Intercultural Studies Program Development, Washington, D.C., 1975.

———. *This Is the Community College.* Boston: Houghton-Mifflin, 1968.

———, ed. *International/Intercultural Consortium Brochure.* Washington, D.C.: AACJC 56th Conference, 1976.

Golden, J. S. "Student Adjustment Abroad: A Psychiatrist's View." *International Educational and Cultural Exchange,* 8 (Spring 1973), 28–36.

Good, H. G. *A History of Western Education.* New York: Macmillan, 1960.

Goodwin, G. L. "The Nature of the Nurture of the Community College Movement." *Community College Frontiers,* 4(3) (Spring 1976), 5–13.

————. *A Social Panacea: A History of the Community-Junior College Ideology.* (ERIC Document Reproduction Service No. ED 093 427), 1973.

Gough, Harrison G., and McCormack, William A. *An Exploratory Evaluation of Education Abroad.* Berkeley: University of California Press, 1967.

Grafton, C. L. "Foreign Student Patterns in American Community Colleges." *Junior College Journal,* 40 (March 1970), 32–33.

Grant, J. P. "United States and the Developing Countries in the New Emerging International Order." *Social Education,* 38 (November 1974), 636–639.

Grant, R. "New Use for an Old Centre of Learning: Abbey of Fiesole, Florence." *The New York Times Educational Supplement,* June 27, 1969, pp. 2101–2103.

Graves, Frank Pierrepont. *A History of Education During the Middle Ages and the Transition to Modern Times.* New York: Macmillan, 1914.

Greenough, R. "Why International Education Year?" *Education Canada,* 10 (March 1970), 16–20.

Griffin, W. H. "World Involvement: Our Continuing Responsibility." *International Educational and Cultural Exchange,* 6 (Winter 1971), 62–76.

Griffith, W. S. "Harper's Legacy to the Public Junior College." *Community College Frontiers,* 4(3) (Spring, 1976), 14–20.

Gunderson, O. D. "Off to Europe's Workshops and Labs; Minnesota Pioneers Again." *American Vocational Journal,* 47 (December 1972), 58–60.

Gunterman, G. "Suggested Procedure for Determining Cultural Objectives." *Hispania,* 59 (March 1976), 87–92.

Guyer, D. L. "International Student and Faculty Exchange." *School and Society,* 98 (March 1970), 178–181.

Hall, W. D. "Towards a European Education System?" *Comparative Education,* 10 (October 1974), 211–219.

Halsey, A. H., and Trow, M. A. *The British Academics.* Cambridge: Harvard University Press, 1971.

Hampton, A. A. "Sense and Sensibility in an International Context." *Comparative Education,* 12 (October 1976), 267–274.

Hans, Nicholas. "The Historical Evolution of Internationalism." In George Z. F. Bereday and J. A. Lauwerys, eds., *The Yearbook of Education—1964: Education and International Life.* New York: Harcourt, Brace & World, 1964.

Harari, M. "International Studies: The Dynamics of Change." *International Educational and Cultural Exchange,* 8 (Spring 1973), 53–60.

Hardin, T. "A History of the Community Junior College in Illinois." Unpublished Doctoral Dissertation, University of Illinois at Urbana-Champaign, 1975.

———. "Joliet: Birth of a College." *Community College Frontiers,* 4(3) (Spring 1976), 21–23.

Harlacher, E. L. *The Community Dimension of the Community College.* Englewood Cliffs, N.J.: Prentice-Hall, 1969.

Harmon, N. W. "In Search of Elisante." *Delta Kappa Gamma Bulletin,* 36 (Winter 1970), 23–28.

Hauska, A. "Austrian Fulbrighter in an American College; Fulbright-Hays Teacher Exchange Program." *International Educational and Cultural Exchange,* 5 (Summer 1972), 49–55.

Hawkins, J. N., and Takata, J. A. "Tenri University: A Religious Approach to International Education." *Peabody Journal of Education,* 49 (July 1972), 300–306.

Hayden, R. L. "Internationalizing Public Education: What the States Are Doing." *International Educational and Cultural Exchange,* 12 (Fall 1976), 3–8.

Hess, G. "Community Colleges and Overseas Academic Programs." *The Community College and International Education: A Report on Progress.* Florida: Brevard Community College, 1981, 36–41.

————. "Internationalizing the Community College." *Intercultural Education in the Two-Year College: A Handbook on Strategies for Change.* Learning Resources in International Studies, 1976, 23–41.

————. "Rockland Community College: 5 Years Later." *International Educational and Cultural Exchange,* 11 (Winter 1976), 3–4.

————. "Trans-Atlantic Adventure for Twenty U.S. Secretaries." *British-American Trade News,* 7 (Spring/Summer 1971), 39–40.

Hickman, W. L. "World Studies for Perspective." *Liberal Education,* 56 (October 1970), 424–431.

Hilton, L. M. "Foreign Study League." *International Educational and Cultural Exchange,* 6 (Winter 1971), 30–37.

Hirsch, Felix H. "The Migration of Scholars in History." *School and Society,* 45 (June 19, 1937).

Ho, Ping-Ti. *The Ladder of Success in Imperial China.* New York: Columbia University Press, 1962.

Holland, K. "Half Century of the Institute of International Education: Only a Beginning." *School and Society,* 98 (November 1970), 426–429.

Holmes, B. "Conceptions of Culture and Society in Educational Research on Individuals." *National Society for the Study of Education Yearbook,* 71 (1972), 193–216.

————. "International Education in Great Britain." *Phi Delta Kappan,* 51 (January 1970), 267–270.

Hopp, J. W. "Specialized Field Work for International Health Education Students: A Survey of Need." *Journal of School Health,* 47 (October 1977), 481–482.

Hu, Chang-Tu, ed. *Aspects of Chinese Education.* New York: Teacher's College Press, 1970.

————. *Chinese Education Under Communism.* New York: Teachers College Press, 1974.

Hu, Chang-Tu, and Beach, B. *Russian-Chinese English Glossary of Education*. New York: Teachers College Press, 1970.

Hull, W. F., and Semke, W. H., Jr. "Assessment of Off-Campus Higher Education." *International Review of Education*, 21(2) (1975), 195–206.

Humphrey, R. A. "International Education and Public Priority." *International Educational and Cultural Exchange*, 5 (Spring 1970), 12–23.

―――, ed. *Universities . . . and Development Assistance Abroad*. New York: The American Council on Education, 1967.

Husen, T. "Does Broader Educational Opportunity Mean Lower Standards?" *International Review of Education*, 17(1) (1971), 77–91.

―――. "Does More Time in School Make a Difference?" *The Education Digest*, 38 (September 1972), 11–14.

Huxley, T. H. "A Liberal Education and Where to Find It." In Frederick Eby and Charles Flinn Arrowood, eds., *The Development of Modern Education in Theory, Organization and Practice*. New York: Prentice-Hall, 1940.

Jacobsen, R. L. "Community Colleges Seek a Global Perspective." *Chronicle for Higher Education*, 15 (November 28, 1977), 5–6.

Jaeckel, H. "Ships and Students at Sea." *International Educational and Cultural Exchange*, 5 (Spring 1970), 68–83.

James, P. E. "Geographic Concepts and World Crises." *Journal of Geography*, 74 (January 1975), 8–15.

Jaramillo, M. L. "Today's Schools Are More Culturally Aware." *Educational Leadership*, 39 (April 1973), 628–631.

Jarrett, James L. *The Educational Theories of the Sophists*. New York: Teachers College Press, 1969.

Jelinek, M. M., and Britlan, E. M. "Multiracial Education." *Educational Research* [Britain], 18 (November 1975), 44–53.

Jessup, F. W. "International Understanding: The Second Concern." *Convergence,* 3(2) (1970), 19–24.

Joel, M., et al. "Non-Sponsored Study Abroad: How to Evaluate." *College and University,* 47 (Summer 1972), 707–711.

Johnson, R. *The French Communist Party Versus the Student Revolutionary Policies in May–June, 1968.* New Haven: Yale University Press, 1972.

Joyce, J. "Educational Reform in Europe: The Role of the U.S. Exchange Program." *International Educational and Cultural Exchange,* 5 (Winter 1970), 36–43.

Kakosteen, Mehdi. *History of Islamic Origins of Western Education A.D. 800–1350, with an Introduction to Medieval Muslim Education.* Boulder: University of Colorado Press, 1964.

Kandel, I. L. *The New Era in Education.* New York: Houghton-Mifflin, 1955.

Kaplan, R. B. "NAFSA in the Mod Mod World." *International Educational and Cultural Exchange,* 6 (Fall 1970), 68–75.

Kasaki, R. H. "Hawaii's Community Colleges—The Past." *Educational Perspectives,* 13(2) (May 1974), 10–11.

Katz, J. "Canada and International Education." *Phi Delta Kappan,* 51 (January 1970), 271–273.

Keenleyside, Hugh L., and Thomas, A. F. *History of Japanese Education and Present Educational Systems.* Tokyo: Hokuseido Press, 1937.

Keller, G. "Hands Across the Sea." *Times Educational Supplement,* March 2, 1973, p. xiii.

Kerr, L. *Foreign Students in Community and Junior Colleges.* Washington, D.C.: American Association of Community and Junior Colleges, 1973.

————, and Diener, T. J. "Two-Year Colleges: New Pioneers." *International Educational and Cultural Exchange,* 10 (Spring 1975), 12–15.

Kibre, Pearl. *The Nations in the Medieval Universities.* Cambridge, Mass.: Medieval Academy of America, 1948.

————. *Scholarly Privileges in the Middle Ages.* Cambridge: Mass.: Medieval Academy of America, 1962.

Kidd, J. Rody. "The First Universities: Takshasila and Nalanda." *Convergence,* 2(3) (1969), 80–83.

————. "Third International Conference [on Adult Education]: Tokyo." *Convergence,* 5(3) (1972), 15–19.

Kindrachuk, M. J. "Some Thoughts on Multiculturalism." *Education Canada,* 15 (Winter 1975), 59–61.

King, E. J. *World Perspectives in Education.* Indianapolis: Bobbs-Merrill Co., 1962.

Knowlton, M. P., and Bianco, D. P. "Proposal: An Institute of International Life at Boston University." *Journal of Education,* 52 (February 1970), 35–49.

Koerner, J. D. *Reform in Education.* New York: The Council for Basic Education, 1968.

Korchuk, S. "Cultural Differences: A Challenge for Education." *Education Canada,* 14 (June 1974), 44–47.

Korshin, O. M. "U.S.-U.S.S.R. Medicooperation." *International Educational and Cultural Exchange,* 9 (Spring 1974), 29–32.

Kuchner, D. Z. "From Florida to Florence." *The School Musician,* 49 (February 1978), 44–45.

La Conte, R. T., and La Conte, C. "Work-Study Exchange for British and American Student Teachers." *Educational Leadership,* 27 (November 1969), 137–139.

La Fountaine, M. "Responsiveness and the Multicultural Society." *Education Canada,* 15 (Winter 1975), 49–52.

Lakin, M. "International Education in the Netherlands." *Intellect,* 101 (January 1973), 245–246.

Lambert, D., and Bressler, M. *Indian Students on an American Campus.* Minneapolis: University of Minnesota Press, 1956.

Lange, D. L., and Jorstad, H. L. "Unique Experience in French Culture: A Cultural Materials Work-in in Bescanon." *The French Review,* 51 (February 1978), 391–397.

Larimer, W. C. "The Genesis of the Junior College Movement." *Peabody Journal of Education,* 54(3) (April 1977), 220–224.

Leach, R. V. *International Schools and Their Role in the Field of International Education.* Oxford: Pergamon Press, 1969.

Leestma, R. "U.S. Office of Education Programs Abroad." *International Educational and Cultural Exchange,* 8 (Fall 1972), 32–45.

Lello, A. J. E. "Grassroots of International Education; Tiverton Grammar School, Devon, England." *Trends in Education,* 29 (January 1973), 52–54.

Lett, Gordon. *Paris and Oxford Universities in the Thirteenth and Fourteenth Centuries: An Institutional and Intellectual History.* New York: John Wiley, 1968.

Levis, C. A., et al. "International Study Program in Recreation." *Journal of Physical Education and Recreation,* 46 (November 1975), 65.

Lippincott, W. T. "From International Evaluation: A Maxim Reinforced." *Journal of Chemical Education,* 52 (April 1975), 205.

Long, H. M. "Factoring Teacher Renewal for a World View." *Social Education,* 34 (May 1970), 534–539.

Lowden, L. M. "The Early History of the American Junior College." *Journal of Educational Administration and History,* 9(1) (January 1977), 32–43.

Lunstrum, Y. "U.S. and Other Great Powers in International Interaction." *National Society for the Study of Education Yearbook,* 68 (1969), 220–249.

Lustig, A. "International Writing Program; Unique in the World; University of Iowa." *International Educational and Cultural Exchange,* 8 (Summer 1972), 33–41.

Lynch, J. M. *Born of Necessity: The Two-Year College in New Jersey.* (ERIC Document Research Information Service No. 134 243), 1970.

Madden, M. A., and Powers, G. F. "Some Non-Academic Aspects of International Education." *National Association of Women Deans and Counselors Journal,* 36 (Summer 1973), 185–189.

Maheu, R. "Commitment to International Education Year 1970." *School and Society,* 98 (Summer 1970), 295–296.

———. "1970. International Education Year." *Convergence,* 3(1) (1970), 12–13.

Male, G. A., and Huden, D. P. "International Education and Western European Countries (Excluding France, Germany and Great Britain)." *Phi Delta Kappan,* 51 (January 1970), 264–267.

Malmquist, E. J., and Grundin, H. U. "International Cooperation in Educational Research." *International Review of Education,* 22 (1976), 339–356.

Marjoram, D. T. E., et al. "European Schools." *Trends in Education,* 2 (Summer 1977), 26–34.

Marrou, H. I. *A History of Education in Antiquity.* New York: Mentor Books, 1964.

Mason, H. R. "Foreign Medical Schools as a Resource for Americans: Mexico and Europe." *Journal of the National Association of College Admissions Counselors,* 15 (November 1970), 16–20.

Massialas, B. G. "Political Socialization in International Perspective." *Educational Leadership,* 27 (November 1969), 155.

Masters, R. D. "Toward Improved Franco-American University Exchanges." *International Educational and Cultural Exchange,* 7 (Winter 1972), 7–15.

Mathies, L., and Thomas, W. G. *Overseas Opportunities for American Educators and Students.* New York: Macmillan, 1973.

McAninch, H. D. "Joliet: 75 Years the Community College." *Community and Junior College Journal,* 46(2) (October 1975), 14–15.

McCormack, W. "Faculty Travel Abroad." *School and Society,* 100 (April 1972), 235.

McIntosh, T. L. "International Wealth Gap and Geography

Instruction." *The Journal of Geography,* 77 (January 1978), 16–24.

McMullen, E. C. "Foreign Lands Made to Order; Volunteers to America Program." *The Journal of Geography,* 69 (October 1970), 420–422.

Medsker, Leland L. *The Junior College: Progress and Prospect.* New York: McGraw-Hill, 1960.

————, and Tillery, D. *Breaking the Access Barriers: A Profile of Two-Year Colleges.* Hightstown, N.J.: McGraw-Hill, 1971.

Melvin, K. "Educational World View." *Journal of Education,* 152 (February 1970), 3–22.

————. "Pax Pedagogica?" *Journal of Education,* 151 (February 1969), 15–21.

Metraux, Guy. "Cross-Cultural Education Through the Ages." *International Social Science Bulletin,* 8(4) (1956), 577–586.

Meyers, J. F. "Multicultural Pluralism: Challenge and Opportunity." *Momentum,* 6 (October 1975), 2.

Michielli, J. A. "Students Abroad Studying Their Own Thing." *Improving College and University Teaching,* 20 (Summer 1972), 160–161.

————. "Study Abroad Adviser on Campus: An Expanding Role." *International Educational and Cultural Exchange,* 5 (Summer 1969), 49–54.

Milne, H. "More Soviet Foreign Links: Longer Stays Abroad." *Times Educational Supplement,* February 28, 1969, p. 642.

Mize, D. "World Education Series Review: Algeria." *College and University,* 52 (Summer 1977), 532–538.

Mogle, H. "Exportation of Ideas, Men and Materials: The Case of Baroda, India." *Viewpoints,* 47 (September 1971), 153–190.

Monroe, Paul. *A Brief Course in the History of Education.* New York: Macmillan, 1924.

————. *Source Book of the History of Education for the*

Greek and Roman Periods. London: Macmillan & Co., 1939.

Mookerji, Radha Kumud. *Ancient Indian Education,* 4th ed. Delhi: Motilal Banarsidass, 1969.

Morgan, E. E., Jr. "Study Abroad: A Process of Adaptation and Change." *International Review of Education,* 21(2) (1975), 207–215.

Morris, R. T. *The Two-Way Mirror.* Minneapolis: University of Minnesota Press, 1960.

Morsch, W. *State Community College Systems: Their Role and Operation in Seven States.* New York: Praeger Publishers, 1971.

Mountford, Sir J. F. *British Universities.* Oxford: Oxford University Press, 1966.

Mueller, S. "International Studies: Crisis and Opportunity." *International Educational and Cultural Exchange,* 5 (Spring 1970), 1–11.

Myers, Edward D. *Education in the Perspective of History.* New York: Harper & Bros., 1960.

Nakosteen, M. *History of Islamic Origins of Western Education A.D. 800–1350.* Boulder: University of Colorado Press, 1964.

Nash, D. "Personal Consequences of a Year of Study Abroad." *The Journal of Higher Education,* 47 (March 1976), 191–203.

————, and Tarr, T. "Stranger Group in an Overseas Study Program." *The French Review,* 49 (February 1976), 366–73. Reply with Rejoinder by O. Andrews, 46 (March 1976), 563–567.

National Association for Foreign Student Affairs. *Adviser's Manual of Federal Regulations Affecting Foreign Students and Scholars.* Available from the Association, 1860 19th Street, N.W., Washington, D.C. 20009.

Nelson, D. N., et al. "They Studied Abroad." *College and University,* 47 (Summer 1972), 288–291.

Neuminster, H. "Education for International Understanding

in the Federal Republic of Germany." *Phi Delta Kappan,* 51 (January 1970), 259–263.

New York State. "Article 126," *New York State Education Law.* Albany, 1962.

Newell, P. "Geneva Notebook." *The New York Times Educational Supplement,* September 24, 1971, p. 80.

Noah, H. J. "Two Contemporary Projects in Comparative Education." *Comparative Education Review,* 14 (October 1970), 262–268.

Norris, C. W., Jr. *The Historically Black Two-Year College: A Forgotten Part of American Higher Education.* (ERIC Document Educational Resources Information Center No. ED 101 801), 1975.

O'Bannon, G. W. "Project Afghanistan: From Experiment to Certainty." *International Educational and Cultural Exchange,* 11 (Winter, 1976), 13.

———. "Project Afghanistan: Undergraduates in Dynamic Cross-Cultural Experiment: University of Pittsburgh." *International Educational and Cultural Exchange,* 8 (Spring 1973), 14–20.

Orr, P. G., and Rockarts, D. G. "Goshen Project in International/Intercultural Education." *National Association of Secondary School Principals Bulletin,* 54 (October 1970), 61–69.

Osborn, J. A., Jr. "Peace Corps: Teachers for the World." *New York State Education,* 57 (January 1970), 21–23.

Osmunson, R. L. "Higher Education as Viewed by College and University Presidents." *School and Society,* 98 (October 1970), 367–370.

Parker, F. "Teaching for World Understanding: A Bibliographical Essay on International and Multicultural Education." *Phi Delta Kappan,* 51 (January 1970), 276–281.

Pasquariello, R. D., and Baroni, G. "Catholic Schools and the Challenge of Intercultural Education: Interview." *Momentum,* 6 (October 1975), 5–11.

Peterson, A. D. C. *A Hundred Years of Education.* London: Gerald Duckworth & Co., 1952.

————. "Program of the International Baccalaureate." *Journal of General Education,* 28 (Winter 1977), 277–282.

Pettiss, S. T. "Whither International Educational Exchange? Social Worker's Perspective and Recommendations." *International Educational and Cultural Exchange,* 6 (Summer 1970), 57–70.

Pfnister, A. O. "Evaluation of Study Abroad Programs for American Colleges and Universities." *The North Central Association Quarterly,* 47 (Spring 1973), 308–318.

————. "Everyone Overseas! Goshen College Pioneers: Study-Service Trimester." *International Educational and Cultural Exchange,* 8 (Fall 1972), 1–12.

————. "Quality Control for Study Abroad Programs." *International Educational and Cultural Exchange,* 8 (Winter-1972–73), 19–35.

Pidgeon, D. "Current Research of the International Association for the Evaluation of Educational Achievement (IEA)." *Comparative Education Review,* 13 (June 1969), 213–216.

Pitman, L. J. "Student Involvement in International Programming." *International Educational and Cultural Exchange,* 8 (Summer, 1972), 42–48.

Plato. *The Portable Plato.* New York: The Viking Press, 1948.

Poignant, R. *Education in the Industrialized Countries.* The Hague: Martinus Nijhoff, 1973.

Postelthwaite, T. N. "International Project for the Evaluation of Educational Achievement." *International Review of Education,* 15(2) (1969), 131–204.

President's Commission on Foreign Language and International Studies. *Report: Background Papers and Studies.* Washington, D.C.: U.S. Government Printing Office, 1979.

Pullias, E. V. "A Historical Perspective: The Land Grant Concept and the Community College Philosophy." *Community College Review,* 3(1) (June 1975), 45–49.

Putman, I., Jr., ed. *The Community College Looks to the 21st Century.* Albany, N.Y.: State Education Department, Foreign Area Materials Center, 1974.

Ramirez, H. M. "Multicultural Education to Make the Nation Greater." *National Association of Secondary School Principals Bulletin,* 57 (May 1973), 138–142.

Rashdall, Hastings. *The Universities of Europe in the Middle Ages,* Vols. 1 and 3, ed. F. M. Powicke and A. B. Emden. London: Oxford University Press, 1936.

Rawat, P. L. *History of Indian Education,* 3rd ed. Agra: Ram Prasad, 1963.

Reimer, M. K. "European Schools: A Venture in International Education." *Phi Delta Kappan,* 54 (April 1973), 550–552.

Reischauer, E. O. *Toward the 21st Century: Education for a Changing World.* New York: Alfred A. Knopf, 1973.

Renner, R. R. "U.S. Aid to Latin American Universities: A Case of Cultural Transfer." *Intellect,* 102 (March 1974), 385–386.

Reubens, B. G. "College and Jobs: International Problems." *Current Issues in Higher Education,* 32 (1977), 182–194.

Richardson, N. "Dateline Sweden: Traditional English Education at a Scandinavian Summer School." *The New York Times Educational Supplement,* August 6, 1976, p. 26.

Robb, F. "Combating Apathy About International Education." *The American Association of Colleges for Teacher Education Yearbook* (1975), 36–40.

Robinson, D. W., ed. *As Others See Us.* New York: Houghton-Mifflin, 1969.

Rockland Community College Bulletin, Rockland Community College, Suffern, N.Y., 1972/73.

Rockland Community College Catalog, Rockland Community College, Suffern, N.Y., 1969/70.

Rodby, W. "To Russia With Song. *The School Musician Director and Teacher,* 41 (March 1970), 42–45; 41 (April 1970), 48.

Roeming, R. F. "Bilingualism and the National Interest. Discussion." *Modern Language Journal,* 55 (May 1971), 314–317.

Rose, C. J. "International Baccalaureate After Ten Years." *Phi Delta Kappan,* 58 (May 1977), 708.

Rosen, S. "U.S.S.R. and International Education: A Brief Overview." *Phi Delta Kappan,* 51 (January 1970), 247–250.

Rosenblatt, H. S. "Dialogue in Newfoundland." *Educational Forum,* 38 (March 1974), 291–294.

Rusch, N. "Master's Degree Program at the University of Salamanca, Spain." *Delta Kappa Gamma Bulletin,* 44 (Fall 1977), 54–58.

Ruth, J. Y., et al. "Opportunities Abroad for AACRAO Members." *College and University,* 45 (Summer 1970), 796–798.

Samuel, R. H., and Thomas, R. Hinton. *Education and Society in Modern Germany.* London: Routledge & Kegan Paul, 1949.

Sanders, I. T. "Private, Non-Governmental U.S. Aid to Education Overseas." *National Society for the Study of Education Yearbook,* 68 (1969), 115–134.

————, and Ward, J. C. *Bridges to Understanding: International Programs of American Colleges and Universities.* New York: McGraw-Hill, 1970.

Sansom, George B. *A History of Japan to 1334.* Stanford: Stanford University Press, 1958.

————. *Japan: A Short Cultural History,* rev. ed. New York: Appleton-Century-Crofts, 1962.

Schairer, Reinhold. *Die Studenten in Internationalen Kulturleben.* Münster i. W.: Aschendorffsche Verlagsbuchhandlung, 1927.

Schenck, E. A., et al. "Credit Recommendations for Study Abroad." *College and University,* 45 (Summer 1970), 434–438.

————. "Educational Exchange: U.S./U.K. Comparison and Interpretation." *College and University,* 46 (Summer 1971), 372–375.

————. "Procedures for Inaugurating Sponsored Study

Abroad Programs." *College and University,* 47 (Summer 1972), 594–604.

Schmidt, H. "En France." *The School Musician Director and Teacher,* 42 (January 1971), 12–13.

Schultz, R. E. "Canada-U.S. Junior College Exchanges." *School and Society,* 100 (January 1972), 5.

———. "Two-Year Colleges Move Toward Global Orientation." *Community College Review,* 5 (Fall 1977), 15–28.

Scott, F. D. *The American Experience of Swedish Students.* Minneapolis: University of Minnesota Press, 1956.

Scully, M. G. "Italy Bars Foreign Students." *Chronicle of Higher Education,* 14 (July 5, 1977), 9.

Scully, M. G. "Notes From Overseas." *Chronicle of Higher Education,* 15 (December 5, 1977), 2.

Sewell, W. H., & Davidsen, O. M. *Scandinavian Students on an American Campus.* Minneapolis: University of Minnesota Press, 1961.

Shannon, E. W. "Europe as a Classroom." *Journal of Health, Physical Education, Recreation,* 45 (February 1974), 94.

Sheffield, J. *Education in Kenya: An Historical Study.* New York: Teachers College Press, 1973.

———, ed. *Road to the Village: Case Studies in African Community Development.* New York: Interbook Inc., 1974.

Sheffield, J., and Diejomack, V. P. *Non-Formal Education in African Development.* New York: Interbook Inc., 1972.

Simonson, M. R. "Global Awareness: A Curriculum Plan for World Study." *NASSP Bulletin,* 61 (October 1977), 75–79.

Sloan, D. *The Great Awakening and American Education.* New York: Teachers College Press, 1973.

———. *Scottish Enlightenment and the American College Ideal* (Studies in Education). New York: Teachers College Press, 1971.

Slocum, J. B., and Warner, R. E. "French Connection." *College and University,* 48 (Summer 1973), 630–641.

Smallwood, J. M. "Teaching Abroad: Where the Jobs Are." *Change,* 9 (August 1977), 18–21.

Smith, R. S. "International Education: A Do-It-Yourself Approach." Junior College Journal, 42 (August 1971), 22–23.

————. "International Education in Australia." *Phi Delta Kappan,* 51 (January 1970), 274–276.

Spaulding, S., et al. *The World's Students in the United States: A Review and Evaluation of Research on Foreign Students.* New York: Praeger Press, 1976.

Springer, V. K. *Recent Curriculum Developments (in France, West Germany and Italy).* New York: Teachers College Press, 1969.

Stagner, R. "Psychology and International Education." *Contemporary Education,* 42 (November 1970), 413–415.

Stangl, J. "Touch of Stramongate." *American Education,* 14 (March 1978), 17–19.

State of New York. *Legislative Manual,* 1975.

State University of New York (SUNY), Central Administration, Office of International Programs, Department of International Education. "Goal Statement" (draft), Albany, N.Y., August 1972, revised March 1975.

————. "Statement on Overseas Academic Programs" (draft), Albany, N.Y., 1976.

State University of New York (SUNY), International Studies and World Affairs Committee. "Position Paper," presented at a Conference on International Education, Syracuse, N.Y., March 25–26, 1976.

State University of New York (SUNY), Office of Vice Chancellor for Academic Programs. *Procedures for the Operations of Overseas Academic Programs by State University Colleges,* Albany, N.Y., November 15, 1975.

Stewart, L. "American Teachers Meet Arabs and Israelis." *Delta Kappa Gamma Bulletin,* 39 (Winter 1973), 9–16.

Stiles, L. J. "Pluralistic Curricular Orientation." *The Journal of Educational Research,* 64 (December 1970), inside cover.

Stock, A. K. "Community Colleges in the United Kingdom." *International Review of Education,* 20(4) (1974), 517–520.

Sturner, W. F. "Reflections on Overseas Study Programs." *International Educational and Cultural Exchange,* 6 (Fall 1970), 45–59.

Sweeney, L. J., et al. "Opportunities for Educational Consultants on Overseas Assignments: Essential Professional Qualifications." *College and University,* 46 (Summer 1971), 422–426.

Szyliowicz, J. S. *Education and Modernization in the Middle East.* Ithaca, N.Y.: Cornell University Press, 1973.

Tagatz, G. E., and Gierl, E. "Implications of International Education: A Challenge for the Future." *Contemporary Education,* 42 (November 1970), 92–93.

Taylor, H. *The World as Teacher.* Garden City, N.Y.: Doubleday, 1969.

Thomas, A. "Somerset Goes to Ghana." *Times Educational Supplement,* September 2, 1977, pp. 26–27.

Thornton, James W., Jr. *The Community Junior College.* New York: John Wiley & Sons, 1972.

Toscano, J. V. "Interim-term World Campus; Study Abroad During January." *International Educational and Cultural Exchange,* 8 (Summer 1972), 23–32.

Townsley, J. "World Is Our Campus." *Times Educational Supplement,* May 11, 1973, p. 77.

Trumbull, D. "Ideal English Language Program: Environmental English: School for International Training, Brattleboro, Vermont." *International Educational and Cultural Exchange,* 5 (Spring 1970), 50–62.

Tyson, L. "Appointment in Kitui Provides Opportunity for Testing Values." *Delta Kappa Gamma Bulletin,* 36 (Spring 1960), 30–34.

Ulich, R. *The Education of Nations: A Comparison in Historical Perspective.* Cambridge: Harvard University Press, 1967.

Urch, G. E. "The Universities, The Teacher and Ethnocentrism." *Journal of Teacher Education,* 21 (Summer 1970), 273–275.

Vaccaro, L. C. "Europeanizing American Higher Education." *Educational Review,* 54 (Summer 1973), 243–245. Reply H. Wasser, 55 (Winter 1974), 65–66.

Van Til, W. "Anyone for International Work?" *Phi Delta Kappan,* 53 (November 1971), 154–155.

———. "Looking From Abroad: Mexico." *Phi Delta Kappan,* 55 (April 1974), 563.

Waggoner, G. R., and Waggoner, B. *Education in Central America.* Lawrence: University of Kansas Press, 1971.

Walden, John W. H. *The Universities of Ancient Greece.* New York: Charles Scribner's Sons, 1909.

Walker, E. L. "On Her Majesty's Service." *Physics Teacher,* 10 (September 1972), 303–312.

———. "What Did You Learn?" *New York State Education,* 56 (May 1969), 30–31.

Ward, D. S. "Needed: Effective Educational Assistance to Latin America." *Educational Digest,* 37 (April 1972), 52–54.

Warfield, J. W. "Teaching at Chiegmai University." *Improving College and University Teaching,* 19 (Winter 1971), 22–25.

Watson, J., and Lippitt, R. *Learning Across Culture.* Ann Arbor: University of Michigan, 1955.

Weakley, J. "Something to Cheer About." *Community and Junior College Journal,* 47(8) (May 1977), 12–14.

Weeks, K. M. "Legal Exchange: The State of the Art." *International Educational and Cultural Exchange,* 7 (Summer 1971), 46–53.

Weidner, E. W. "U.S. Institutional Programs in International Education." *Phi Delta Kappan,* 51 (January 1970), 239–243.

Wells, H. B., and Arnold, D. B. "American University in World Affairs." *National Society for the Study of Education Yearbook,* 68 (1969), 135–152.

Wierusowski, Helene. *The Medieval University: Masters,*

Students, Learning. Princeton, N.J.: D. Van Nostrand, 1966.

Williams, G. L. "Beyond the Classroom: Life Experiences in the Field." *The Clearing House,* 45 (October 1970), 81–85.

Wood, E. A., and Wood, R. W. "Group Projects Abroad: Programs in India for American Educators." *Delta Kappa Gamma Bulletin,* 44 (Fall 1977), 27–33.

Wood, J. M., ed. "Global Hunger and Poverty: Symposium." *Social Education,* 38 (November 1974), 628–688.

Wooten, C. C. "International Studies and the Disciplines." *School and Society,* 98 (November 1970), 413–415.

Wykes, O. "International Education in France." *Phi Delta Kappan,* 51 (January 1970), 256–258.

Zirkel, P. A. "Legal Vicissitudes of Bilingual Education." *Phi Delta Kappan,* 58 (January 1977), 409–411.

Index